Christianity and the Outsider

Christianity and the Outsider

A Lawyer Looks at Justice *and* Justification

JAMES W. GEIGER

RESOURCE *Publications* • Eugene, Oregon

CHRISTIANITY AND THE OUTSIDER
A Lawyer Looks at Justice *and* Justification

Copyright © 2012 by James W. Geiger. All rights reserved. Except for brief quotations in critical publications or reviews, no part of this book may be reproduced in any manner without prior written permission from the publisher. Write: Permissions, Wipf and Stock Publishers, 199 W. 8th Ave., Suite 3, Eugene, OR 97401.

Resource Publications
An Imprint of Wipf and Stock Publications
199 W. 8th Ave., Suite 3
Eugene, Or 97401
www.wipfandstock.com

ISBN: 978-1-62032-067-9
Manufactured in the U.S.A.

Unless otherwise indicated, Bible quotations are taken from the New American Standard Bible (NASD) version of the Bible—Copyright 1973 by Foundation Press. Illustrations by JC Creative Services of Pompano Beach, FL

This book is dedicated to Mary, who is my wife, confidant, and proofreader extraordinaire, to my parents Mallory and Mildred Geiger who were privy to the new covenant in Christ, to Ted and Ruth Prince who were privy to God's covenant with Israel, and to their son and my friend Charles Prince who is privy to both of these great covenants.

In God you come up against something which is in every respect immeasurably superior to yourself. Unless you know God as that—and, therefore, know yourself as nothing in comparison—you do not know God at all. As long as you are proud, you cannot know God. A proud man is always looking down on things and people: and, of course, as long as you are looking down, you cannot see something that is above you.

C. S. Lewis, *Mere Christianity*

Contents

Preface ix

PART I: THE SCANDAL OF EXCLUSIVITY
   1. Confession of a Christian Insider 3
   2. Dilemma of the Outsider 9
   3. Reclaiming Divine Revelation 17

PART II: DIVINE INITIATIVES
   4. Revelation as Creation: In the Beginning 29
   5. Revelation as Law: Human Accountability 35
   6. Revelation as Christ Event: Divine Redemption 43
   7. Revelation: Looking Back 52

PART III: THE CASE FOR THE CONSTANT CHRIST
   8. Revelation: A New Perspective 61
   9. The Relativity Model and Constant Value 77
   10. Constant Value and the Constant Christ 87
   11. Faith *of* Jesus Christ 97
   12. Forgiveness: The Why and the How 112

PART IV: SPECIAL REVELATION: LIFE WITHIN A COVENANT
   13. Special Revelation: Jewish Insiders *before* the Cross 125
   14. Special Revelation: Christian Insiders *after* the Cross 131

PART V: GENERAL REVELATION: LIFE WITHOUT A COVENANT
   15. General Revelation: Non-Jewish Outsiders *before* the Cross 139
   16. General Revelation: Non-Christian Outsiders *after* the Cross 149
   17. Paul's Olive Tree: Insiders and Outsiders on the Same Tree? 159
   18. From Accountability To Repentance To Forgiveness 173
   19. No Other Name Under Heaven 184
   20. Conclusion 189

Appendix 193
Bibliography 203

Preface

Christianity and the Outsider tells the story of a perfect God rescuing imperfect people from their imperfection. It offers some fresh ideas regarding God's relationship with outsiders and makes some new connections between science and religion. However, all of the proposals reaffirm the biblical narrative that says: God is, he created the heavens and the earth, and he revealed himself in and to his creation through the faithfulness of Jesus Christ.

I want to clarify at the outset that I am neither a Universalist nor a proponent of "Christian Universalism." I am fully committed to the gospel message that says Christ's atonement is the only means of reconciliation between God's perfection and humanity's sinful imperfection. And I am equally committed to Jesus' statement that says, ". . . repentance for forgiveness of sins should be proclaimed in His name to all the nations, beginning from Jerusalem" (Luke 24:47).

The Bible quotes are from my copy of the *New American Standard Bible* (NASB 1975), unless otherwise indicated. Similarly, the Greek and Hebrew word studies are from *The Complete Word Study Old Testament* (AMG 1994) and *The Complete Word Study New Testament With Greek Parallel* (AMG 1992), also unless otherwise indicated. Occasionally, I use brackets [. . .] or *italics* within biblical quotations. Obviously, these inserts are not part of the translation. The *italics* are used to show my emphasis and the [bracketed inserts] have been added to clarify my understanding of the text.

I use analogies and legal illustrations as well as poetry to focus attention on ideas that are too heavy for my lightweight prose. All of the poetry is original except for a few quotes where I give third party attribution.

Preface

Christianity and the Outsider is the sequel to *The Gospel According to Relativity* that was published in 2005. The first book used some special terms to explain what I call a new model of understanding, and some of those terms have been carried over to this new book. To help clarify the meaning of these terms, I have added an Appendix to this book and inserted a reference to the Appendix the first time I use each new term. I hope the background set forth in the Appendix will help explain the new model.

In the final analysis, I am trying to build a bridge between the new covenant's insiders and outsiders in order to remind my fellow insiders that God's perfection reaches beyond the horizon of human understanding.

Part I
The Scandal of Exclusivity

Insiders and Outsiders

1

Confession of a Christian Insider

There is a fundamental difference between "insiders" and "outsiders." Insiders draw circles around themselves and "their kind" in order to exclude outsiders from a variety of privileges. Some forms of exclusion are related to race, class, and ethnicity, but the most controversial ones are associated with religion.

In 1958 I began a journey that exposed both the privileges of insiders and the problems of outsiders. I was a White Anglo-Saxon Protestant (WASP) and a senior at a Christian college in the segregated South. I needed a summer job, but I wasn't worried because I was an insider. I had lined up a construction job through my father who was a superintendent for a company that built bridges. Having just gotten married, I was in a position to support my new bride and to save money for my last year in college. I was not only a WASP but also an upper middle class son of privilege—a 24-carat insider.

A new awareness of my insider status dawned on me that summer as I worked next to a young man who was also recently married. George was a black laborer instead of a white college boy. We were part of a small rigging crew that included a truck crane and an operator. Our job was to demolish the old McArthur Causeway that connected Miami and Miami Beach. Section by section, we worked our way across Biscayne Bay, knocking out the asphalt roadway, removing the structural steel beams, and loading them onto trucks to be hauled away.

My awareness of George's outsider status was both positive and negative. On the positive side, we became friends. I learned that we were the same age and had the same hopes and dreams for our families. Working with George, I found that he was smart, honest, and hard working. I also learned that he lived out of town. He rode a Greyhound bus from Perrine to Miami each day and then transferred to a city bus in order to get to work. He wore clean clothes on the bus, changed into work clothes on the job site, and then reversed the process on his way home. I admired his thoughtfulness toward his fellow passengers, but confess that I would not have changed clothes before and after each bus ride if I had been in George's position.

On the negative side, I found that I was helpless to eliminate or even mitigate the bigotry and the use of the "N" word that were heaped upon George by the crew finishing the new bridge. On one occasion a man tried to dehumanize George by saying, "He's not George; he's just a damn n . . . " I have often wondered what became of my friend after that summer. I have also wondered how my philosophical and theological ideals would have been affected if I had been the outsider instead of the insider.

My insider status allowed me to finish college, attend law school, and enter the legal profession. I became an FBI agent, served as a private lawyer, and was elected to the office of prosecuting attorney. In addition to having a legal career, I taught law related courses and Great Books at a local college and led Bible studies at my church. But I have never forgotten my early exposure to the gulf that separates insiders and outsiders.

That experience over fifty summers ago changed my life and prompted me to seek a deeper understanding of the insider/outsider phenomenon. The temptation, of course, is to theorize about differences like the racial tensions between Caucasians and people of color, religious distinctions between Christians and non-Christians, and today's conflicts between Western civilization and the Islamic world.

I have found that attitudes are often softened when abstract categories become personal relationships like my friendship with George and my work with Jewish colleagues. Most conservative pastors are unequivocal when they generalize about eternal damnation, but they tiptoe around the particulars when they counsel with Messianic Jews regarding the fate of traditional parents and grandparents. The truth is that insider/

outsider issues are more difficult to deal with when they involve personal relationships.

Personally, I have struggled with the apparent inconsistency that says I should love non-Christian outsiders as they are, but that I should also try to change them into Christian insiders. Jesus, himself, said, "You have heard that it was said, 'You shall love your neighbor, and hate your enemy.' But I say to you, love your enemies, and pray for those who persecute you" (Matt 5:43–44). But he also said, "Go therefore and make disciples of all the nations, baptizing them in the name of the Father and the Son and the Holy Spirit teaching them to observe all that I commanded you . . . " (Matt 28:19–20).

Clearly, Christians have commitments to both insiders and outsiders—But how are we to fulfill our responsibilities on both sides of the street? Where would one begin sorting over two thousand years of troubles between Christians and non-Christians? I think we have to start at the very beginning.

Christianity originated in Israel twenty centuries ago when a group of Jewish outsiders acknowledged Jesus of Nazareth as Israel's promised Messiah. The religious and political forces in Israel opposed the "Jesus people" from the very beginning. Later, the Roman Empire joined the opposition and eventually engaged in a series of horrendous persecutions.

Of course, Emperor Constantine's conversion to Christianity in 312 CE and the tolerance required by the Edict of Milan in 313 CE changed everything. It eliminated the systematic persecution of Christians and eventually turned Christianity into the official religion of the Roman Empire. Beginning with the Council of Nicaea in 325 CE, the new respectability helped bring about a series of church councils, and these councils hammered out a Christian consensus that soon dominated the Western world. In less than three hundred years, these religious outsiders had become religious insiders.

In 1054 CE a church split occurred that divided the Orthodox Catholics in the East and the Roman Catholics in the West. Eastern Orthodoxy then developed around cultural identities that resulted in the Greek Orthodox Church, the Russian Orthodox Church, and so forth. Five hundred years later, the Protestant Reformation broke the Roman Catholic dominance in the West and ushered in an era of multiple churches and denominations.

Christianity and the Outsider

Christians are now scattered all over the earth, and they represent an array of beliefs—from fundamentalists, to conservatives, to moderates, to liberals, to radicals. Notwithstanding all the theological differences, that fourth century consensus still carries considerable weight, and it continues to identify Christians as insiders and non-Christians as outsiders.

Statisticians now estimate the world's population to be about seven billion people, but only about two billion of them have any connection with Christianity. Who are these Christian "insiders," and what is their relationship with non-Christian "outsiders"?

Even more important, what is God's relationship to the five billion outsiders who have not heard, do not understand, or have rejected Christianity? Are *all* of these outsiders separated from God and destined for eternal damnation?

This book is the confession of a Christian insider who grieves over the traditional enmity between Christians and non-Christians and grapples with the idea of eternal damnation for non-Christian outsiders who have not heard or understood the gospel.

Admittedly, Christians can be judgmental when generalizing about non-Christians. However, the insider/outsider phenomenon is not limited to the Judeo-Christian tradition. Indeed, it is further complicated by role reversals in the Middle East and other parts of the world. For example, in the Arab world, the followers of Muhammad (570–632 CE) are the insiders, and Christians are the outsiders. Similar inversions exist with other religions as well as with secular humanism. The insider/outsider classifications are reversed, but the conflict remains the same. Furthermore, there are people on both sides who avoid building bridges between insiders and outsiders.

There is a limited sense in which even the Bible seems to work against building bridges between insiders and outsiders. The Scripture says God's "covenant" with Israel goes back nearly four thousand years to Abraham, and Christianity's "new covenant" goes back two thousand years to Christ and the early church. These two covenants correspond to the Old Testament/New Testament division in the Bible, and they account for the exclusive message of each tradition, that is, the exclusivity of Israel's insider status as well as the exclusivity of Christianity's insider status.

At the same time, the Bible reveals God's compassion toward outsiders, a compassion that should foster the "bridge building" process. In the

Old Testament, the Jewish prophet Jonah preached repentance to non-Jewish outsiders in Nineveh. Both the people and their leader repented, and God showed compassion toward them. But there is no indication that the outsiders of Nineveh became part of God's covenant with Israel. In the New Testament we find the apostle Paul preaching the gospel to religious outsiders in Lystra and Athens, and many of them eventually became Christian insiders. However, as I will discuss later, Paul seems to suggest that God had compassion for the "generations gone by" who had been excluded from the biblical covenants (Acts 14:16).

These are some of the issues that have prompted me to dig deeper, to revisit Scripture passages that deal with outsiders, and to reassess the insider/outsider dilemma in the Judeo-Christian tradition.

As the son of a bridge builder, I am suggesting the possible existence of a biblical "bridge" between Christians and non-Christians. The proposed bridge is based upon a spirituality that says human existence should be understood in relationship to *constant value*—that is, eternal value that is independent of human existence and does not change with the passing of time.

The idea of constant value is not new. In the world of science, constant value is seen in the constant speed of light as in $E=mc^2$. In the secular world and in various world religions, constant value is understood as an abstraction that manifests itself as love in personal relationships and as justice in social relationships. In the Christian world, constant value is made concrete in the person of Jesus Christ who is the same "yesterday and today, yes and forever" (Heb 13:8)—In other words, the constant Christ of the Bible does not change from time to time and place to place just as the constant speed of light does not change from time to time and place to place.

Experientially, the universality of love and justice is seen in the fact that children experience love and recognize injustice long before they are integrated into religious, economic, and/or political groups. The same universality is seen in the nursery where toddlers are oblivious to skin color until they are later exposed to racial and cultural prejudices.

Theologically, the constant Christ confirms the existence of universal value and normalizes the relationship between insiders and outsiders. As we shall see in the following chapter, Jesus used a Samaritan outsider in Luke 15 to teach compassion to Jewish insiders. Also, in Matthew 25 Jesus concluded his earthly ministry with a parable in which "the King"

Christianity and the Outsider

identifies himself with the outsiders rather than the insiders. The King's attitude toward outsiders and Christianity's relationship with these outsiders are themes that will be explored throughout this book.

2

Dilemma of the Outsider

What about the outsiders who have never heard the gospel, the African tribesman who died before the missionaries arrived, and the Messianic Jew who grieves for family and friends who did not or will not accept his Jesus as their Messiah?

These are the "insider/outsider" questions that have always haunted the Judeo-Christian tradition. C.S. Lewis referred to Christianity's insider/outsider problem as the "scandal of exclusivity."[1]—That is, Christianity claims that Jesus Christ is the *only* means of reconciliation between God's perfection and humanity's imperfection. In the spirit of full disclosure, I confess that I am a Christian insider who is fully committed to the exclusivity of the gospel story. But I am troubled by the dilemma on the other side and have tried to study the "scandal" from the perspective of the outsider.

Should Christian insiders reexamine their attitude toward outsiders? The answer to that question must be understood in both historical and contemporary terms. Historically, Christianity has had to "reinvent" itself from time to time as it moved from the early church, through the Constantine conversion, to the fall of Rome, to the medieval period, to the Reformation, to the Americas, and on to modernity. Now, as the church moves into the twenty-first century, it must reinvent itself once again in

1. Burson, *C.S. Lewis & Francis Schaeffer*, 200.

order to reaffirm the truth of the gospel in a postmodern world. Like it or not, Christianity is faced with a world population that is not only changing demographically but also expanding exponentially.

Christianity usually discusses God's relationship with insiders and outsiders in the context of special revelation and general revelation:

Special revelation acknowledges that both Jews and Christians are theological insiders. Israel's "covenant" looks forward to the coming of Messiah, while "new covenant" Christians look back to Messiah as well as forward to his second coming. (See Appendix Sec. 1.00)

General revelation brings Judeo-Christian insiders face to face with the outsiders who "live and move and have (their) being" (Acts 17:28 KJV) without the special benefits that are inherent in those two biblical covenants. (See Appendix Sec. 2.00)

What does the Bible say about the people left outside the biblical covenants? I seek to answer this question by identifying Jesus Christ not only as the traditional Messiah but also as the "constant Christ" who is the common denominator between the insiders of special revelation and the outsiders of general revelation.

LIVING WITHOUT A COVENANT

If the covenant with Israel and the new covenant in Christ are *special revelations* from God, then non-Jews are strangers to the first covenant and non-Christians are strangers to the new covenant. Eternal consequences flow from the fact that these outsiders have been left out of God's covenants. Indeed, the damning consequence of exclusion from the traditional covenants has caused some people to wonder whether God may have revealed himself to these strangers in some general way, that is, through general revelation.

As we examine special and general revelation in the discussion that follows, an underlying issue will be whether Christian theology is justified in limiting God's forgiveness to the insiders who are privy to the traditional covenants or whether divine forgiveness is capable of reaching out beyond the finite horizon of human understanding.

Jesus, himself, may have foreshadowed general revelation in a parable that addressed the issue of knowing or not knowing the master's will. He said, "And that slave who knew his master's will and did not get ready or act in accord with his will, shall receive many lashes, but the one who did not know it, and committed deeds worthy of a flogging, will receive but few. And from everyone who has been given much shall much be required; and to whom they entrusted much, of him they will ask all the more" (Luke 12:47–48). Dare we look at both sides of the issue and say, ". . . from everyone who has been given much shall much be required" and ". . . *from everyone who has been given less shall less be required*"?

The Bible is clear that God desires to bless the whole world. The idea of blessing the world is found in both the Old Testament and the New Testament. In Genesis, for example, the Lord said to Abram, "And in you *all* the families of the earth shall be blessed" (Gen 12:3). In the fourth gospel, Jesus said, "For God so loved *the world*, that He gave His only begotten Son" (John 3:16). In the Pauline epistles, the apostle closed his three chapter discussion of the insider/outsider problem (Jewish/non-Jewish) with a statement that, "God has shut up *all* in disobedience that He might show mercy *to all*." Then he launched into a hymn of praise celebrating the wisdom and knowledge of God and acknowledging his own limitations—"Oh, the depth of the riches both of the wisdom and knowledge of God! How unsearchable are His judgments and unfathomable His ways!" (Rom 11:32–33).

As an insider to the new covenant, I feel morally obligated to reexamine my relationship with covenant outsiders, and to seek a deeper understanding of God's grace.

As a starting point, I would point out that today's communication and transportation technologies have created unprecedented contacts between covenant "insiders" and "outsiders" and forced both sides to confront their differences in a more forthright manner. The multitude is even more "multitudinous," and the relationships between insiders and outsiders are more complex than ever before.

At the same time, we should acknowledge that the spiritual needs of insiders and outsiders are the same today as they were two thousand years ago. The mandate to love both your friends *and* your enemies is the same today as it was when Jesus told the story of the Samaritan outsider who went out of his way to care for the Hebrew insider. In telling that story, Jesus was fully aware that the Samaritans were not part of God's continuing covenant with Israel, yet he chose to use the outsider to teach compassion to a group of covenant insiders (Luke 10:30–37).

Luke's parable regarding the Samaritan outsider is particularly compelling in view of the Matthew 25:31–46 narrative in which the King "separates the sheep from the goats." Jesus said, "*all* the nations" will be gathered before the "Son of Man" and be separated into a righteous group and an accursed group. The King will identify the righteous as "blessed of My Father," and they will "inherit the kingdom prepared for you from the foundation of the world."

But notice how Jesus characterizes "righteous" people. First, no distinction is made between covenant insiders and outsiders. Second, righteousness is not associated with an insider's understanding of the gospel, as such, but with a person's compassion for the disenfranchised who are variously described as hungry, thirsty, strangers, naked, sick, and in prison. Third, as mentioned earlier, the King identifies himself with the outsiders—*I was* hungry, thirsty, a stranger, etc., and you ministered *to Me*. Indeed, "to the extent that you did it to one of these brothers *of Mine*, even the least of them, you did it *to Me*."

Then the King will turn to those on his left and say, "Depart from Me, accursed ones, into the eternal fire." *I was* hungry, thirsty, a stranger, etc., and you *did not minister to Me*. The parable has a devastating potential for covenant insiders because it says they could find themselves separated from God and his saving grace. The irony is that some "religious" insiders could eventually be reclassified as accursed outsiders. The parable is particularly sobering when one realizes that it is Jesus' final lesson. All that remains in Matthew's gospel is the closing narrative regarding the crucifixion and the resurrection. So what is the nature of God's relationship with insiders and outsiders?

COVENANT VS. NON-COVENANT RELATIONSHIPS

I begin the reexamination of God's relationship with covenant insiders and outsiders with an illustration from the law of contracts. Admittedly, most contracts are for the benefit of contractual insiders. For example, in the purchase of a home, the insiders are the people who are selling the house and the people who are buying the house. They are the actual parties to the agreement or "covenant." By the same token, a biblical covenant is primarily the story of covenant insiders.

Historically, the Judeo-Christian covenants make a radical distinction between covenant "insiders" (*special revelation* for Jews and later Christians) and covenant "outsiders" (*general revelation* for the rest of the world). Indeed, Old Testament outsiders (non-Jews) and New Testament outsiders (non-Christians) have been generally viewed as eternally separated from the saving grace of God and destined for a godless hell.

Biblically speaking, God used the "covenant" with Israel as a vehicle for a special revelation to Jewish insiders, and the "new covenant" in Christ as a vehicle for a special revelation to Christian insiders. The issue is whether God might have used the traditional covenants to benefit both covenant insiders and outsiders?

In discussing these two historical covenants, let us assume, for example, that God and Israel (A and B) have an initial relationship, and that God and Christianity (A and C) have a subsequent relationship. Obviously, Jews would have benefits and responsibilities under the first covenant, and Christians would have benefits and responsibilities under the new covenant.

However, suppose God (A) entered into a covenant relationship with Israel (B) with the intent to benefit Christians (C) in the future—even though they were strangers to the initial covenant. To further complicate the situation, what if God (A) later entered into a new covenant relationship with Christianity (C) with the intent also to benefit the rest of humanity (D)—even though these outsiders were strangers to both covenants?

In other words, could God have entered into a Jewish covenant that would eventually benefit non-Jewish outsiders and then a Christian covenant that would eventually benefit non-Christian outsiders? Gentile Christians would have to affirm the first scenario—but most would deny the second. How can we account for that contradiction?

THIRD PARTY BENEFICIARIES

As mentioned earlier, most contracts are for the benefit of the insiders who are actual parties to a particular arrangement. However, the initial parties can enlarge the contractual picture by designating an outside party as a "third party beneficiary."

Christianity and the Outsider

A life insurance policy is a classic example of a "third party beneficiary contract." A parent (the first party) and an insurance company (the second party) can enter into an arrangement or covenant (the insurance policy) with the parent designating the children as beneficiaries (the third party).

The parent pays the premium and is entitled to some benefits during his or her lifetime, but the real value is the death benefit that goes to the children when the parent dies—*even though these "third party beneficiaries" were strangers to the original covenant.* The company is the temporal conduit charged with carrying out the "earthly" father's intent.

Since God is omnipotent, he certainly has the power to designate outsiders as "third party beneficiaries." Indeed, the insurance analogy seems to illustrate the possibility that God may have provided an eternal benefit for some outsiders—*even though they were strangers to the new covenant in Christ.* Is it possible that the "heavenly" Father provided the new covenant in order to benefit both covenant insiders *and* outsiders, and if so, how?

On the God-side of the new covenant, the two aspects of God's perfection are seen as he deals with humanity's sinful imperfection: God-as-Father (A) demonstrated *perfect justice* by holding his fallen children accountable for their sin—And God-as-Son (A) demonstrated *perfect love* by paying the price for that sin. Speaking theologically, the Son made "atonement" or justified human sin so the Father could grant "forgiveness" to repentant sinners.

In the Christmas story, God-as-Son intervened in human history and became a fellow-heir with each human being (Rom 8:17)—But in the Easter story, he paid the price for each person's sinful imperfection. "Incarnation" means the eternal Son entered into the temporal realm, and "crucifixion" means the Son paid the ultimate "premium" for humanity's "eternal-life-insurance." As the apostle Paul explained it, Christ:

> ... existed in the form of God, [but] did not regard equality with God a thing to be grasped, but emptied Himself, taking the form of a bond-servant and... being found in appearance as a man, He humbled Himself by becoming obedient to the point of death, even death on a cross. Therefore also God [the Father] highly exalted Him [the Son], and bestowed on Him the name which is above every name, that at the name of Jesus every knee should bow, of those who are in heaven, and on earth, and under the earth, and

that every tongue should confess that Jesus Christ is Lord, to the glory of God the Father (Phil 2:6–11).

On the human-side of the new covenant there is a band of people who are blessed with having received the "good news" of the gospel story—They are the *ecclesia*, the "called out" church of Jesus Christ. The Bible says these Christian insiders are to "contend earnestly for the faith which was *once for all delivered to the saints*" (Jude 3). As "the bride of Christ," the church is the custodian of the gospel message and is charged with the mission of spreading the good news throughout the world. Indeed, even the "gates of Hades [or death] shall not overpower it" (Matt 16:18). The church of Jesus Christ is the temporal conduit charged with carrying out the "heavenly" Father's intent.

On one hand, *special revelation* examines the Son's atonement and the Father's forgiveness from the perspective of the Christian insider. Some of these covenant insiders find favor with God and are identified as "a Chosen Race, a Royal Priesthood, a Holy Nation" (1 Pet 2:4–9). The apostle Paul said these people "... are being led by the Spirit of God, these are the sons of God . . . you have received a spirit of adoption as sons by which we cry out, 'Abba! Father!'" (Rom 8:14–15). Unfortunately, some insiders have access to the new covenant, but they are not adopted into the household of faith. Like Judas Iscariot or perhaps the young ruler of Luke 18, some insiders are privy to the gospel message, but their rebellious state of mind separates them from God's saving grace.

On the other hand, *general revelation* examines the Son's atonement and the Father's forgiveness from the perspective of the outsider. According to the apostle Paul, insiders and outsiders have general accountability *for sin*—"For there is no partiality with God . . . for all have sinned [and] the wages of sin is death" (Rom 2:11, 3:23, 6:23). But what does this impartiality have to say about outsiders and the possibility of a general remedy *from sin*?

If we affirm God's "special revelation" to the covenant insiders who are privy to the biblical covenants, then intellectual honesty requires that we at least consider the possibility that God may have provided a "general revelation" for covenant outsiders. Indeed, if Christian theologians push the envelope ever so slightly, they might realize that the "third party beneficiary" idea from the law of contracts provides a finite picture of a third party dynamic that might be at work in the new covenant.

Christianity and the Outsider

The question is whether atonement and forgiveness are available at least to some of the outsiders who have been excluded from the biblical covenants. More specifically, did Christ die for, and is God's forgiveness available to any of the outsiders who are not privy to the new covenant?

I am suggesting that if God-the-Father's *perfect justice* can condemn an outsider who has no appreciation for the new covenant, then perhaps God-the-Son's *perfect love* is able to redeem that outsider even though he or she has no appreciation for the new covenant. In other words, I am:

1. Challenging Christian "insiders" to identify with covenant "outsiders" as the Master did in Matt 25:45 and to empathize with them as the apostle Paul did in Acts 14 and 17,

2. Making a biblical argument to support the possibility of salvation for non-Jews before the cross and non-Christians after the cross, and

3. Using general revelation to make non-Christians part of the biblical story.

But, as Mary said to the angel in Luke 1:34, "How can this be?"

3

Reclaiming Divine Revelation

Revelation is the process whereby deity is manifested in human history. In its most basic form, the infinite God created finite creatures, and then revealed himself in and to his creation. As Augustine famously said, *"You have made us for yourself, O Lord, and our hearts are restless until they rest in you."*[1]

DIVINE PERFECTION

Is divine revelation still a viable issue in postmodern America? Admittedly, secularism has made massive inroads in Western culture. But I would argue that most Americans still have a religious perspective. America's continuing spirituality is seen in "The Narcissus Survey" that *The New Yorker* published a few years ago. The article entitled "Fearless Inquiry Into Whatever" covered the whole spectrum from the general public on "Main Street," to the affluent folks on "Easy Street," to the culturally elite on "High Street." The survey determined that when people were asked, "Do you believe in God?" most people said, "Yes." The affirmation was made by 92 percent of the people on Main Street, 90 percent of the people on Easy Street, and 61 percent of the people on High Street.

---

1. Augustine, *The Confession of Saint Augustine*, 11.

The idea of revelation accounts for humanity's intuitive awareness of God and God-talk in general. The intuition overcomes the barriers of time, place, and situation, and causes people either to submit to or to rebel against the God of the universe. Indeed, revelation means every person on earth has some kind of relationship with the Creator whether he or she understands it or not.

The Judeo-Christian tradition says, "And God created man in His own image . . . " (Gen 1:27). In other words, an infinite and perfect Creator created finite creatures in his perfect image. Therefore, some degree of freedom is part of that image. God's creation made us free, but freedom exposed us to disobedience and "the Fall" (Gen 3). The law of gravity causes people to fall *down* from a higher to a lower position. By the same token, the Fall caused humanity to fall *down* from perfection to imperfection, and sin has cascaded *down* through history ever since. The apostle Paul confirmed humanity's finite trajectory when he said, "all have sinned" and later concluded that "the wages of sin is death" (Rom 3:23, 6:23).

On one hand, God's *perfect justice* required accountability for humanity's sinful imperfection—The Genesis story says God held humankind accountable for sin from the very beginning. Accountability was and is necessary in order to avoid injustice.

On the other hand, God's *perfect love* provided a remedy for humanity's imperfection. With the creation narrative, Adam and Eve "fell down" from perfection to imperfection. But with the gospel narrative, God provided a remedy whereby an imperfect creature can "fall up" to God's forgiveness.

Why should finite imperfection be redeemed and made acceptable to divine perfection—because "God so loved the world" (John 3:16). God loved his creation so much that he underwrote a plan to redeem humanity from its imperfection. Indeed, God's plan to redeem humankind existed even before the imperfection appeared on the scene—the plan had been put in place from "the foundation of the world" (Eph 1:4).

Biblically, the first phase of special revelation affirms the Jewish tradition wherein God revealed himself as having a covenant relationship with the people of Israel. A second phase of special revelation was predicted in Jer 31:31 and later confirmed as a "new covenant" wherein God revealed himself in the person of Jesus Christ. Both Jews and Christians acknowledge God's "covenant" with Israel, and Christians acknowledge the existence of the "new covenant."

Both covenants speak of God's continuing relationship with humanity and of humanity's continuing accountability to God. And they both indicate that our accountability to God must be understood in the context of the Fall and humanity's redemption from the Fall. We have *rebelled* against God, we are *accountable* for our rebellion, but God has provided a *remedy* for our insubordination.

However, is God's remedy limited to covenant "insiders," or do the biblical covenants hold out the possibility that God's special revelation may also have general implications for covenant "outsiders"?

Special revelation is related to both Judaism and Christianity. It is unique in that nearly two thousand years of Hebrew history had elapsed between Abraham and the birth of Christ. Now an additional two thousand years have passed, and during this time there have been continuing developments in the relationship between Judaism and Christianity. Yet each one is still playing a major role on the world stage. Over the centuries, both Jews and Christians have suffered great persecution, but each one is still understood as a "particular way of being religious and so a particular interpretation of religion."[2]

Undoubtedly, God knew that if he restricted the manifestation of himself to one particular culture, pride would cause that culture to assert a proprietary interest in his work. He solved the problem by creating an inclusive classification model wherein two categories are able to encompass the whole world: that is, Jews and non-Jews as well as Christians and non-Christians. Of course, the classification model can also be generalized as uniform and non-uniform.

God's revelation is inclusive because in revealing himself to Jews and non-Jews, he included everyone in the world. The inclusiveness is like the landowner who said he didn't want to own all the land in the world—He just wanted to own all the land that touched his land. Even so, both Israel and Christendom have tried at times to claim God's grace as an exclusive franchise. Jews and Christians understand historical events very differently, but each tradition believes itself to have received a special revelation from God:

---

2. Gilkey, "A Retrospective Glance at My Work," 35.

Traditional Jews believe Holy God entered into a special covenant with the people of Israel whereby he promised to bless them and to send an *anointed one* who would be a blessing to the whole world.

Traditional Christians affirm the existence of the Jewish covenant as well as a "new" covenant that reaches out to the non-Jewish world. They believe that after two thousand years of preparation within Jewish culture, God revealed himself *as the anointed one* in the person of Jesus of Nazareth—the Christ event.

I use the term "Christ event" to emphasize that there is more involved here than the thirty plus years in the lifespan of the historical Jesus. The New Testament speaks of the Father-Son-Holy Spirit reality as predating the Bethlehem story and continuing for eternity. The eternal dimension of the Christ event is seen in the fourth gospel that says, "In the beginning was the Word, and the Word was with God, and the Word was God . . . And the Word became flesh, and dwelt among us, and we beheld His glory, glory as of the only begotten from the Father, full of grace and truth" (John 1:1,14).

Of course, some modern people have abandoned the idea that God is and that he has revealed himself in the person of Jesus Christ. But there are many others who continue to acknowledge that Christ was and is God's ultimate revelation to humankind. Indeed, if traditional Christianity is true, then the Christ event as manifested through the Judeo-Christian tradition has universal implications for *all* people.

The Bible says, ". . . the Word of God is living and active and sharper than any *two-edged sword,* and piercing as far as the division of soul and spirit, of both joints and marrow, and able to judge the thoughts and intentions of the heart. And there is no creature hidden from His sight, but all things are open and laid bare to the eyes of Him with whom we have to do" (Heb 4:12–13).

If God has revealed himself to *all* humanity as the Scripture says, then I would have to describe revelation as a two-edged sword:

One edge of the sword would identify Christ as God's *special revelation.* He was predicted in Jewish tradition, proclaimed in the Christian tradition, and embraced as the primary force in Western civilization. Indeed, Western culture was once referred to as "Christendom"— *Christ's king*dom.

The other edge of the sword would indicate that God's *general revelation* is a universal expression of God's grace, and that it has divine implications for all people—Jews and non-Jews as well as Christians and non-Christians.

If God used the double-edged idea of special and general revelation to reveal himself to his creation, then it doesn't matter whether Christians understand *how* it happened, and it doesn't matter whether non-Christians understand *that* it happened.

I have struggled to come up with an illustration that would paint a word picture regarding the relationship between special and general revelation, and the best I can do is tell the story of the Denver Water Board. It seems that there were Colorado visionaries in the 1800s who saw that a growing Denver was going to need a lot of water. They not only obtained extensive "water rights" to the Rocky Mountain snow that falls each year but also developed a special plan to bring the melted snow to Denver. They built a reservoir high up in the Rockies to collect the melt as it flowed downward and a huge pipeline to funnel the water from that reservoir to an even larger reservoir on the outskirts of the city. Even today, the second reservoir holds the water until it is needed by the thirsty citizens of Denver.

Of course, the rest of the snow also melts, and the law of gravity carries it down the mountains. However, this water follows the *general* terrain of the mountains instead of the *special* plan developed by the Denver Water Board. The same force carries all the water downhill, but some is channeled to serve a special purpose, and the rest serves a general purpose—that is, creating lakes and streams and supporting plant and animal life.

In like manner, special revelation brings the living water of God's grace down from his holy hill to Israel's covenant "reservoir," channels it through the atonement of Jesus Christ, and finalizes the process in Christianity's new covenant "reservoir." The point is that special revelation was and is a unique plan that serves humanity's need for redemption. The reservoir in the mountains and the one near the city illustrate the two-step covenant process that God used in special revelation. He used the initial covenant with Israel not only to focus on the law of accountability but also to reveal the promise of redemption (Isa 43:1–2, 53:11–12). Later, when Jesus made atonement for sin, God used the new covenant to make the good news of the gospel message available to the rest of the world (Matt 28:18–20).

Obviously, creation applies to all people, and the Bible teaches that the law's accountability for sin applies to all people. The only question is whether there is a sense in which the Son's atonement and the Father's forgiveness are available to all people—That is, to both covenant insiders and outsiders. If "there is no creature hidden from His sight" (Heb 4:13), then Jews and Christians as covenant insiders should not try to corral God within their special covenants.

The prophet Isaiah understood the problem when he said, "Woe to the one who quarrels with his Maker—An earthenware vessel among the vessels of earth! Will the clay say to the potter, 'What are you doing?' Or the thing you are making say, 'He has no hands'" (Isa 45:9)? Covenant insiders are "earthenware vessels" among all the other "vessels of earth," and we should be slow to pass judgment on what "the potter" is doing. In the words of an old western song, God seems to be saying, "Don't fence me in."

HUMAN IMPERFECTION

Divine perfection cannot tolerate fallen imperfection. Wrong rubs against right like bone against bone— if that which is *perfect* were combined with the *imperfect*, then perfection, as such, would no longer exist. For example, if you have a glass of water and a tiny drop of poison is added, then it's no longer drinkable. If you have perfection, and a small imperfection is introduced, then you no longer have perfection. So how can divine perfection tolerate human imperfection?

Hebrew and Christian Scriptures agree that humanity has a primal problem. Humans were created in the image of God, but they have fallen from that lofty position. Indeed, human experience confirms the dark side of human nature without any reference to biblical texts. Even a cursory review of human history, especially the mechanized warfare of the twentieth century, reveals that every era and every culture has suffered carnage, mayhem, and injustice. The problem is that all living organisms are engaged in a struggle to survive, and competition leads to self-centeredness and the drive to overcome obstacles.

Human nature, however, is an enigma because self-centeredness in human beings is different from other species. On one hand, human beings have animalistic propensities that are natural to all species. On

Reclaiming Divine Revelation

the other hand, the Judeo-Christian teaching says humans were created in God's image, and that they can *overcome* their animalistic propensities through Christ. Furthermore, *failure to overcome* their self-centered nature is characterized as rebellion against God—It's what the Bible calls sin. How can a perfect God have any involvement with imperfect human beings?

The apostle Paul grappled with the ambiguity of human nature throughout his life, especially in the Book of Romans. He was an approving spectator at Stephen's martyrdom and a lethal crusader on the road to Damascus. But his Damascus Road conversion changed him, and he eventually played a pivotal role in the development of Christianity. Years later, however, a mature Paul would confess that his imperfection was a continuing problem—"For that which I am doing, I do not understand; for I am not practicing what I would like to do, but I am doing the very thing I hate" (Rom 7:15). In spite of Paul's struggle with the ambiguity of human nature, the Book of Romans is sometimes described as the Bible's purest gospel. As such, it provides a good starting point for our discussion of human nature.

Paul's writing acknowledges God's perfection, but it also confirms humanity's imperfection. The apostle says each individual is accountable for his or her sinful imperfection, and then explains how God, himself, provided a remedy for human sin. In fact, the first three chapters of Romans provide a template for the discussion of humanity's imperfection, as well as God's remedy for that imperfection.

In Romans chapter 1, Paul says sin is universal, and every person is accountable for his or her own sin. The rationale goes all the way back to the Genesis story where Adam and Eve enjoyed the freedom of having been created in the image of God, but they misused their freedom and were held personally accountable for their disobedience. Their primal innocence was canceled out, making them representative of all the sinful people who would live after them. The apostle said *all* people know God (v. 19, 21), but they have exchanged the image of an *incorruptible* God for a *corruptible* image of their own making (v. 23). In their self-centeredness they worship and serve the "creature" instead of the "Creator" (v. 25).

My wife has an engaging wall plaque that hangs in our kitchen. It's interesting because it illustrates the ultimate nature of sin. The plaque shows a cat with his paw on the edge of a fish bowl and a caption that says: "In a cat's eyes, all things belong to cats." The human tendency is to ignore

Christianity and the Outsider

God and act as if "all things belong to humans." We know better, but we defy God by exchanging his glory for our own "glory"—a poor imitation. The sin is the same whether one has an objective thought pattern where "God is up in heaven" or a subjective thought pattern where "God is down in my heart." What does the Bible mean when it says sin is universal and every person is accountable for his or her sin?

In chapter 2, Paul explains the universality of human accountability by making it inclusive, that is, applicable to both Jews and non-Jews.

He acknowledges Jewish spirituality but says traditional religiosity does not absolve one of personal accountability to God. Paul even concedes that Jews have a special relationship with God, but he denies that God is partial to Israel. In fact, he says the knowledge and truth of the Mosaic Law creates added responsibility rather than special privilege. Paul says, ". . . you bear the name Jew, and rely upon the Law, and boast in God" (Rom 2:17) [but] "he is not a Jew who is one outwardly; neither is circumcision that which is outward in the flesh. But he is a Jew who is one inwardly; and circumcision is that which is of the heart, by the Spirit, not by the letter; and his praise is not from men, but from God." (Rom 2:28–29). Individual Jews have a spiritual accountability for sin that extends beyond their participation in God's covenant with Israel and beyond their knowledge of the Mosaic Law.

Non-Jews are also accountable to God. Indeed, they have the same spiritual accountability that the Jews have—and without the full benefit of the Mosaic Law and the prophets. "For all who have sinned without the [Mosaic] Law will also perish without the Law; [but] . . . when Gentiles who do not have the Law do instinctively the things of the Law, these, not having the Law, are a [general] law to themselves, in that they show the work of the Law written in their hearts, their conscience bearing witness, and their thoughts alternately accusing or else defending them, on the day when according to my gospel, God will *judge* the secrets of men *through Christ Jesus*" (Rom 2:12, 14–16).

Chapter 3 of Romans opens with a reaffirmation of humanity's universal accountability to God. Paul spoke directly to the Jews in chapter 2, and then used chapter 3 to reemphasize the fact that *all* people are equally accountable to God whether they are Jews or non-Jews. For example, the apostle asks rhetorically if Jews, with their biblical pedigree, are better than non-Jews, and then says, "Not at all; for we have already charged that both Jews and Greeks are all under sin" (Rom 3:9). He then quoted Psalm 14:

> There is none righteous, not even one;
> There is none who understands,
> There is none who seeks for God.

The apostle made a universal indictment of human nature when he said the law makes the whole world "accountable to God . . . for through the Law comes the knowledge of sin" (Rom 3:19–20). God created perfect but finite people, and gave them a degree of freedom—but they abused their freedom and fell from perfection to imperfection. In Rom 3:20, Paul identified the law as the vehicle for universal accountability.

However, in Rom 3:21 he shifted from general accountability to what might be described as God's "rehabilitation program." Biblically speaking, it is the plan of redemption that will be discussed in greater detail throughout this book.

The point here is that God's perfect justice holds all human beings accountable for sin, but his perfect love has provided a remedy from sin. As I will explain in the next three chapters, God revealed himself in three general initiatives that impact all people, for all time, and in all places: The first initiative was creation. The second initiative was the law that makes all humanity accountable to God. And the ultimate initiative was the Christ event, which is the "power of God for salvation to every one who believes, to the Jew first and also to the Greek [or non-Jew]" (Rom 1:16).

Part II
Divine Initiatives

———————

The Christ Event

The Law

Creation

4

Revelation as Creation: In the Beginning

Creation was God's first initiative. Both the medieval philosopher Anselm and the modern scientist Albert Einstein were concerned with the same question, "Why is there something rather than nothing?"

GOD'S FIRST INITIATIVE

God's first initiative is pictured in the Genesis account, which says, "In the beginning God created the heavens and the earth . . . " Without preface or argument, the Bible simply proclaims that God is, and that he took the initiative in creating the whole universe. How could the creative initiative be otherwise? Artists take the initiative when they carve statues, and scientists take the initiative whether studying ants or zebras. Indeed, can you imagine an artist who has the potential to paint the perfect picture, or the inventor who has the power to create the ultimate invention, and he or she does nothing?

God's creative initiative was one of a kind—creation *ex nihilo* (out of nothing). God not only created "the heavens and the earth," but he also created beings "in his own image" (Gen 1:1, 27). He fashioned a responsive creature that was even *free to rebel* against its Creator. A comparable situation in a cartoon strip would call for the creation of a cartoon

Christianity and the Outsider

character that could spit in the face of the cartoonist and maybe even pick his pocket.

Of course, any discussion of creation is a conundrum like "Which came first, the chicken or the egg?" Did the eternal God create the universe out of nothing or is the universe eternal and, therefore, not in need of a creator? "*Some*thing" cannot come from "*noth*ing," so either God as creator is eternal or the universe has an eternal existence. Indeed, simple logic says one can assume either the existence of an eternal creator or the existence of an eternal universe, but not both. So which is it?

The biblical worldview is that God is eternal. He is the alpha and omega, the uncaused cause, who "created the heavens and the earth." (Gen 1:1). This view has a long track record in the Judeo-Christian tradition. Furthermore, even a cursory study of other cultures reveals that most of them have creation stories in which God was instrumental in bringing the universe into existence.

However, there is another perspective that views the universe, itself, as eternal. Admittedly, some ancients believed the universe was eternal, but a whole new approach has developed in the modern era as scholars have sought to reshape Western civilization in a way that minimizes and even eliminates the Judeo-Christian idea of divine revelation.

The philosopher Matthew Stewart recently analyzed the idea of worldview in a book that describes the seventeenth century as ". . . an age of transition—the time in which the theocratic order of the medieval era ceded to the secular order of modernity."[1]

On one hand, Wilhelm Leibnitz (1646–1716) was a German-Christian philosopher who sought to justify Christianity's traditional view. He was an extrovert with his wigs, fancy dress, and upward social mobility, but he was also a highly regarded intellectual. He invented calculus independent of Isaac Newton's work, built the first calculating machine, and wrote on a wide variety of subjects including science, politics, and philosophy. Most important, however, was his theological position as a defender of the faith, including the idea of a transcendent God who had created the universe and all that we understand as nature.

On the other hand, Baruch Spinoza (1632–1677) was a Dutch-Jewish philosopher who developed nontraditional views at a rather early age. His ideas were contrary to Jewish tradition and were deemed atheistic

---

1. Stewart, *The Courtier and the Heretic*, 15.

by the Christian tradition. In the 1500s, Spinoza's family had been part of a thriving Jewish community in Portugal, but the Portuguese Inquisition forced them to either convert or flee. The family eventually landed in Holland where they attained financial security and were able to continue their Jewish traditions. Spinoza was born in Amsterdam and educated under the guidance of Amsterdam's leading rabbis. However, his rationalist and pantheistic ideas clashed with Jewish orthodoxy and caused him to be expelled from the Jewish community.

Understanding Spinoza's philosophical system is beyond the scope of this study, but his theory that the "stuff" of the universe is eternal and that human reason has an unlimited capacity to understand this "stuff" is the central issue in deciding whether a holy God "created the heavens and the earth." According to Stewart, "Spinoza did not invent the modern world, but he was perhaps the first to observe it well. He was the first to attempt to answer the ancient questions of philosophy from a distinctly modern perspective. In his philosophical system, he offers a concept of God befitting the universe revealed by modern science—a universe ruled only by the cause and effect of natural laws, without purpose or design."[2]

Why did Spinoza write "Nature" with a capital N and "God" with a capital G? He capitalized both words as morally equivalent—He referred to "Nature" and "God" as the one and only "Substance" in the universe. In other words, Spinoza's "Nature" not only deals with birds and bees and trees, but it generalizes nature, itself, including the "the nature of light" and the "nature of man."[3]

The definitive issue of Spinoza's Nature or God is that this "Substance" is wholly accessible to human reason alone—"there is nothing ultimately mysterious in the world; there are no inscrutable deities making arbitrary decisions, and no phenomena that will not submit to reasoned inquiry—even if that inquiry is inherently without end; in short, that there is nothing that cannot be known—even if we do not necessarily know everything."[4]

For Spinoza, this "all in all" is the eternal essence or "stuff" of a universe that is without beginning or end.

---

2. Ibid., 15.
3. Ibid., 158.
4. Ibid., 158–159.

NATURE AND MODERNITY'S CLAIMS

Spinoza and his intellectual successors worship at the modern altar of "human reason." Indeed, he was the forerunner of a long line of Enlightenment figures who would pay homage to human reason as the door to ultimate reality. Modern reason has an illustrious family tree. We see its genealogy in the point/counterpoint between the "I think, therefore, I am" rationalism of Rene Descartes (1596-1650) and the "blank tablet" empiricism of John Locke (1632-1704) where knowledge comes only through experience and the senses. Eventually these two conflicting points of view found a synthesis of sorts in the work of Immanuel Kant (1724-1804) where human reason ("pure reason") was understood as the connecting agency between temporal experience (*phenomena*) and eternal reality (*noumena*).

Spinoza's "modern" idea was that there is only one kind of eternal "Substance" in the universe, and that human reason is the ultimate way to understand this ultimate "stuff"—And his successors have been legion. Indeed, as we enter the twenty-first century, we need to realize that some things haven't changed very much since the seventeenth century.

Today, Richard Dawkins, scientist, professional atheist, and the best selling author of *The God Delusion*, perpetuates Spinoza's legacy, except he has dropped any pretense regarding the divine. Dawkins and fellow atheist Julian Baggini agree that ". . . *there is only one kind of stuff* in the universe, and it is physical; out of this *stuff* comes minds, beauty, emotion, moral value—in short the full gamut of phenomena that gives richness to human life."[5]

The vital question is whether these atheists have painted themselves into a corner. In other words, they have staked out a rather narrow position when they declare that there is only "one kind of stuff" in the universe and that human reason is the ultimate resource for testing the heights and depths of that universe.

Allowing no room for human limitations, much less humility, Dawkins's pronouncements echo the early relativism of Protagoras (c. 490-421 BCE) who said, "Man is the measure of all things."[6] Instead of being modern, Spinoza, Dawkins, et al. give voice to the ancient dogma of

---

5. Dawkins, *The God Delusion*, 14.
6. Palmer, *Looking At Philosophy*, 49.

Revelation as Creation: In the Beginning

Protagoras and the other Greek Sophists who were advocating relativism twenty-five hundred years ago.

The truth of the matter is that Dawkins's high regard for human understanding is not consistent with the twentieth century scholarship that says human understanding is limited rather than unlimited.

In her book *Incompleteness: The Proof and Paradox of Kurt Godel*, philosophy professor Rebecca Goldstein identifies Kurt Godel (1906–1978), Albert Einstein (1879–1955), and Werner Heisenberg (1901–1976) with this new wave of scholarship where Godel used mathematics to establish "limits of formal systems." His "incompleteness" theorem suggests the existence of meaning that extends beyond the horizon of human reason. Goldstein says Godel's work was not as well known as the work of his more famous colleagues, however:

> This man's [Godel] theorem is the third leg, together with Heisenberg's uncertainty principle and Einstein's relativity, of that tripod of theoretical cataclysms that have been felt to force disturbances deep down in the foundation of the 'exact sciences.' The three discoveries appear to deliver us into an unfamiliar world, one so at odds with our previous assumptions and intuitions that, nearly a century on, we are still struggling to make out where, exactly, we have landed.[7]

But not Dawkins—He has a nineteenth century certainty about where *he* has landed! In spite of Godel's *"incompleteness" theorem*, etc., Dawkins has a *"completeness" obsession* that says there is only "one kind of stuff" in the universe and that human understanding is an unlimited vehicle for understanding this "one kind of stuff."

However, Dawkins undermines his own "certainty" when he says, "If there is something that appears to lie beyond the natural world as it is now imperfectly understood, we *hope* eventually to understand it and embrace it within the natural."[8] (My Emphasis) When Dawkins "*hopes* eventually to understand," he allows *uncertainty* to sneak into his physical system like a person without a ticket might stowaway on a cruise ship. In the final analysis, it appears that Dawkins is absolutely certain about his uncertainty!

---

7. Goldstein, *Incompleteness*, 135–136, 21–22.
8. Dawkins, *The God Delusion*, 14.

The formal logic of Godel's mathematics even suggests an irony regarding Dawkins's use of "*delusion*" in the title of his book—*The God Delusion*. Goldstein says: "As one textbook on psychopathology puts it: '*Delusions* may be systematized into highly developed and rationalized schemes which have a high degree of internal consistency once the basic premise is granted . . . *The delusion* frequently may appear logical, although exceedingly intricate and complex.'"[9] [My emphasis]

What could be more "highly developed," "rational," "logical," "intricate and complex" than the science and technology that Dawkins and his friends have fused with modern relativism in order to claim that humanity is the "measure of all things"?

Instead of a "God delusion," one might say the real "delusion" is Dawkins' use of his own rationality to validate his view of human rationality. His misperception is that human rationality alone is capable of determining that there is "only one kind of *stuff* in the universe," and that at some point human rationality will be capable of knowing everything.

If there is only one kind of stuff, then all human beings, including Dawkins, are made up of *that stuff*. Furthermore, if Dawkins is functioning within *that* system, then how can he "get outside *that* system to determine whether or not it is rational"? Godel's mathematical logic proves that Dawkins cannot absolutize his own position—He cannot validate human rationality by using his own rationality.

The sad reality is that humanity's rebellion against God merely confirms the peculiar relationship that exists between the Creator and his creation. God created us in his image, yet we are free to rebel against him. Indeed, the late modern/postmodern reality is that people continue to foment new forms of rebellion. As we shall see in the next chapter, God provided a second initiative in order to hold people accountable for all kinds of rebellion whether ancient or contemporary.

---

9. Goldstein, *Incompleteness*, 204–205.

5

Revelation as Law: Human Accountability

The law was God's second initiative. The law acknowledges the sovereignty of the infinite creator and establishes the accountability of his finite creation. Furthermore, it provides a universal frame of reference for right and wrong.

GOD'S SECOND INITIATIVE

God's second initiative is seen in the accountability narrative played out in the lives of Adam and Eve as well as Cain and Abel. We see the difference between right and wrong and learn that God holds people accountable for wrong choices. People like Abel find favor with God, but rebels like Cain are separated from God.

The law's complexity is seen in an eternal accountability that encompasses all people, for all times, and in all places. It is inclusive, restrictive, and simultaneously positive and negative:

The law is *inclusive*. We know "the law" existed before the Mosaic Law because people were accountable to God long before Moses came on the scene. Murder was murder before the Mosaic Law said, "Thou shall not kill." However, with the unfolding of God's covenant relationship with Israel, "the Law" took on a special codification and played a unique role in the lives of the Israelites. As we shall see later in a more detailed discussion of God's covenants, the law has a dual application. The law has special impact on the Jews by virtue of God's covenant with Israel and the Mosaic Law, but it also has an extended impact on non-Jews because the Bible says, "... they show the work of the Law written in their hearts" (Rom 2:15).

Therefore, it is incumbent upon both Jews and non-Jews to obey the law. Indeed, it is a serious misnomer to suggest that people break the law. The problems of dysfunctional families, the shattered dreams of prison inmates, and the death and devastation of war testify to the brokenness of the human race—We don't break the law; the law breaks us!

To the Jew who defies the Mosaic Law, the apostle Paul says, "your circumcision [under the Mosaic Law] has become uncircumcision" (Rom 2:25). In like manner, when non-Jews obey the general law that is "written in their hearts," their "uncircumcision [is] regarded as circumcision" (Rom 2:15, 26). In this context, Paul is not talking about the Gentile who converts to Judaism. A non-Jewish convert to Judaism would have to deal with the requirements of the Mosaic Law just like ethnic Jews. Instead, Paul is saying Jews and non-Jews are equally accountable to God—non-Jews are accountable to God even if they have never heard of the Mosaic Law.

The inclusive nature of the law is seen in the fact that all societies from tribal groups, to city-states, to national governments have rules. The rule of law is usually a formal legal system, but within families and tribes it might be an elemental sense of right and wrong. The rudimentary sense of right and wrong is seen in the fact that children know the difference between fair or unfair or just and unjust long before they know anything about the law or religion. What is the difference between law and religion? The apostle Paul said, "for through the Law comes the knowledge of sin" (Rom 3:19–20), then added, "But now apart from the Law the righteousness of God has been manifested..." (Rom 3:21–22). In other words, the law identifies the wrong, and God reveals the right.

The law is *restrictive*. Whether described as God's laws, governmental laws, or informal customs and conventions, laws are restrictive, and no one likes restrictions. In the wild, animals roam about with unrestricted freedom. Indeed, nature allows predators to attack their prey at will. Like other animal species, each person has a "natural" desire to do whatever strikes his or her fancy. However, the law imposes its restrictions, and people who function outside the rules of society are referred to as "outlaws."

Domesticated animals are trained to live within restrictions, and people are also supposed to live within certain restrictions, especially legal restrictions. Unfortunately, law-abiding people are forced to deal with the outlaws who refuse to comply with the civil and criminal laws that regulate society. Print and broadcast media saturate our lives with daily reports regarding the uninhibited behavior of people who disregard their obligations to society. Having been forced to hold the outlaws accountable for their unlawful behavior, society then tries to walk the fine line between punishment and rehabilitation.

The law is *positive*. Admittedly, the law has positive aspects. Jesus said his followers should "render unto Caesar the things that are Caesar's and to God, the things that are God's" (Matt 22:21).

Paul pointed out the law's positive impact on society when he said every person is subject to governmental law and that to engage in unlawful conduct is to oppose the ordinances of God. "Do what is good, and you will have praise . . . But if you do what is evil, be afraid; for it [the government] does not bear the sword for nothing" (Rom 13:3-4).

Peter also provided a positive caveat regarding the law when he said, "Submit yourselves for the Lord's sake to every human institution, whether to a king or the one in authority, or to governors as sent by him for the punishment of evildoers and the praise of those who do right. For such is the will of God that by doing right you may silence the ignorance of foolish men. Act as free men, and do not use your freedom as a covering for evil, but use it as bondslaves of God" (1 Pet 2:13-16).

It should be noted that the positive side of the law is not limited to beneficial governments. Peter and Paul had experienced the severity of oppressive governments in Jerusalem and throughout the Roman Empire, so their words are not limited merely to "good" governments. Godly people must show respect for the law even when they are forced to live under the rule of a bad government—I suppose the "order" of a totalitarian government is better than the murder and mayhem of total anarchy.

The law is also *negative*. Having alluded to the positive side of the law, the apostle Paul spent most of his time explaining that the negative side of the law identifies sin. As previously mentioned, instead of making us better by solving humanity's sin problem, the law accentuates the sin problem, ". . . for through the Law comes the knowledge of sin *(hamartia)*" (Rom 3:20). The biblical meaning of *hamartia* is "to miss the mark" in one's relationship with God. The problem is comparable to an archer whose arrow misses the target. Spiritually speaking, everyone has missed the mark of God's perfection. Therefore, instead of affirming one's "goodness," the law confirms that every individual has fallen short of God's perfection *to some extent*.

All human beings are law-breakers in the sense that no one is capable of obeying every facet of human law, much less divine law. When people avoid the more egregious violations of society's laws, we say they are law-abiding. These "law-abiding" folks may be "less bad" than career criminals, but the truth is that they, too, are outlaws to some extent. A person does not become "good" by being "less bad" than another person; that is, by minimizing the degree to which he or she violates the law. It is God's perfection that exposes and condemns our imperfection. The law highlights our imperfections. It is like a teacher's red pencil that identifies one's mistakes, or the mounted spotlight on a police cruiser that probes dark alleys looking for criminals. The law reveals that no matter how "good" we think we are, we fall short of God's perfection.

The situation is like a man who puts on a white suit in a dimly lit bedroom. Then as he eats breakfast under the kitchen lights, he notices some soiled spots on his suit. Later, as he walks outside into the bright sunshine, he realizes that his "white" suit is downright dirty. The closer we are to the light, the more we realize we are unclean. As one becomes aware of God's infinite glory, he becomes more aware of his finite imperfection. Conversely, the more highly one regards himself, the farther his pride separates him from God's glory.

Whether positive or negative, the law is a divine process that not only encourages good behavior, but also causes a person to realize that he or she has fallen short of God's perfection. In dealing with these two aspects of the law, it is especially important to realize that an individual's accountability to God is not a conditional "if/then" arrangement—as in, *if* the son mows the lawn and takes out the trash, *then* he is entitled to his allowance. Some people mistakenly think that *if* their lives balance out with more good than bad, *then* they will be accepted as "good" in the eyes of the Lord. Divine perfection and human imperfection result in a non-negotiable arrangement where sinful imperfection cannot be bargained away.

Revelation as Law: Human Accountability

As mentioned earlier, "through the law comes the knowledge of sin" (Rom 3:20). The law does not make me good for the part that I obey; rather, the law shows that I have a problem because of the part that I disobey. In all my years of driving an automobile, I have never had a policeman pull me over and congratulate me for having obeyed the lawful speed limit, but I have had more than a few officers hold me accountable for the part of the speed limit that I violated.

NATURE PLUS ACCOUNTABILITY

It is a misnomer to refer to nature as the "law of the jungle" because the jungle does not have systemic "rules and regulations." In the animal kingdom, a predator is limited only by its instinct and prowess. In human society, however, restrictions distinguish between legal and illegal activities. With humans, the law fences off animal-like propensities as unacceptable.

The beauty of the King James translation says it all—"The law *frameth* the mischief" (Ps 94:20). Indeed, the Bible reveals the essence of "legal" restrictions:

1. The law *limits*—"through the law comes the knowledge of sin" (Rom 3:20);
2. The law *limits universally*—"all have sinned and fall short of the glory of God" (Rom 3:23); and
3. The law *has universal consequences*—"the wages of sin is death" (Rom 6:23).

The law is like the fortress walls of an ancient city. Inside the walls, the law sets *limits* and imposes consequences on those who disregard its limitations. However, outside the walls there are *no limits,* and each person is "free" to do as he or she pleases.

Obviously, there are trade-offs with both positions: *Inside* the "city limits" there is some loss of autonomy, but one gains a degree of security, civility, and predictability. *Outside* the city wall, one is "free," but that "freedom" entails a fearful scenario. Indeed, if there is no law, then everyone is theoretically free to do as he or she pleases.

As an abstract concept, the idea of total freedom is enticing. My mind soars with excitement as I contemplate the things I could do if I were released from all restrictions and obligations. However, if I were free to do as I please—others would also be free to do as they please, even free to impose their will on me. The fact is that such freedom is the fearful reality that Dostoyevsky (1821–1881) must have had in mind when Ivan Karamazov in *The Brothers Karamazov* suggested that if there is no God, then everything is permitted. We might paraphrase by saying, "If there is no law, then everything is permitted." Power and anarchy then become the endgame.

Various thinkers have tried to resolve the freedom vs. restriction dilemma with political ideas based on self-imposed "social contracts." Indeed, modern democracy is based on the social contract ideas of Thomas Hobbes (1588–1679), John Locke (1632–1704), Jean-Jacques Rousseau (1712–1778), and others. Each of these writers argued that the "consent of the governed" had been established when people in a fictional "state of nature" entered into the social contracts under which they agreed to be governed.

More recently, John Rawls (1921–2002) suggested a "theory of justice" that used a hypothetical social contract where decisions regarding the law would be made behind a "veil of ignorance." That is, social justice and fairness would be assured if everyone had to agree on a system of justice without knowing what his or her position would be in such a system— For example, would one be male or female, black or white, rich or poor, etc.[1] Rawls said such a government would be administered by "principles that characterize a well-ordered society under favorable circumstances."[2] Does Rawls' idealistic perspective have a realistic application?

Unfortunately, governments are complex systems that defy predictability. Instead of being "well-ordered" systems functioning "under favorable circumstances," government is messy and volatile. Experience shows that even when social relationships are rearranged as in the French Revolution or more recently with the Soviet Union, Cuba, or Rwanda, the oppressed group can become the new oppressor. In the final analysis, when a theoretical plan becomes a concrete system, it is subjected to all the positive and negative vicissitudes of human behavior, especially the abuse of power. Only the "long-arm" of the law can protect the innocent from the "strong-arm" of a predator. And when predators get control of the legal machinery such as the legislative process of making the law, the

---

1. Rawls, *A Theory of Justice*, 12.
2. Ibid., 397.

Revelation as Law: Human Accountability

executive process of enforcing the law, or the judicial process for interpreting the law, the general public is headed for some dark days.

A pride of lions attacking an antelope and a man eating a steak occupy different positions in nature's food chain, but there is a sense in which they are both predators. However, where the lion is a natural predator, human beings must overcome their animalistic propensity if they are to fulfill their destiny of having been created in the image of God. The law, whether divine or civil, recognizes the imperfections that are inherent in human nature and tries to deal with nature's proclivity by establishing minimum standards. The problem occurs when (not if) a person disregards God's standards and succumbs to nature's predisposition. Indeed, there are not enough police officers and prison guards on earth to sustain civil society if massive numbers of people disregard the innate principles of right and wrong.

Of course, one must be aware that he has a problem before he can contemplate a solution to the problem. A wolf is not aware of the admonition to "love your neighbor" when it kills sheep, and a toddler is not aware of being selfish when it takes another child's toy. The wolf never changes, but when the child becomes aware of the difference between right and wrong, then he or she has crossed the Rubicon from blamelessness to civil and eternal accountability.

Acknowledging that one has violated the laws of civil society is the first step toward rehabilitation under governmental penal codes. Likewise, to acknowledge one's alienation from God is the first step toward divine reconciliation. God's law provides the threshold for humanity's accountability by spotlighting disobedience. It focuses on disobedience like an x-ray detects a bone fracture. When the law is violated, the mask of autonomy falls, and we understand that we are accountable to God for our sinful imperfection. As Mark Twain famously said, "Man is the only animal that blushes. Or needs to!"[3]

In terms of general accountability, *all* people, whether ancient or modern, are accountable to God because all people are "under the law" (Gal 4:4–5). Of course, the general law is expressed in different ways for different peoples. Whereas the Mosaic Law was codified as part of God's special relationship with Israel, the Gentiles "show the work of the law written in their hearts" (Rom 2:15).

---

3. Twain, *Following the Equator*, 117.

Christianity and the Outsider

God created us as human beings, and he holds us accountable for disregarding divine law. But, as we shall see in the next chapter, he has also provided a final initiative to rescue us from our rebellious imperfection.

6

Revelation as Christ Event: Divine Redemption

The Christ event was God's ultimate revelation. The universality and pageantry of the Christ event is summed up in Isaiah's use of the name Immanuel—"God is with us" (Isa 7:14).

GOD'S REDEMPTIVE INITIATIVE

The Christ event is God's ultimate initiative. God created time and space, and then he revealed himself in time and space. In other words, God revealed himself to his creation through the mystery of the Christ event, an event in which Jesus Christ was the *medium* of divine revelation as well as the *message* that was revealed. Jesus was the medium through which God intervened in space-time and the message that was communicated through his birth, death, and resurrection.

Seven hundred years before Christ, Isaiah said God was preparing Israel for the birth of a unique messenger (Isa 7:14, 53:1–12). As prophesied, ". . . she gave birth to her first born son; and she wrapped Him in cloths, and laid Him in a manger, because there was no room for them in the inn . . . today in the city of David there has been born for you a Savior, who is Christ the Lord (Luke 2:7, 11).

Christianity and the Outsider

The apostle Paul later said, "But when the fullness of time came, God sent forth His Son, born of a woman, born under the law, in order that He might redeem those who were under the Law . . . " (Gal 4:4). Creation is confirmed when a child is "born of a woman"; justice is confirmed because every child is "born under the law"; and the Christ event is confirmed because divine redemption is possible for "those who were under the law."

The grand theme of the biblical story is that God *created* moral agents in his own image, that he holds these agents *accountable* for their insubordination, and that he *forgives* those who surrender their prideful self-importance. God's perfect justice holds all people accountable for sin, but his perfect love forgives those who respond to his initiatives.

> Image of God
> Being created in the image of God made me free,
> But in the wonder of my freedom I found sin.
> Being born under the law made me accountable,
> But by the grace of God I received forgiveness.
> The beauty of forgiveness is seen in Christ's birth.
> The pathos of forgiveness is seen in his cross.
> The victory of forgiveness is seen in his empty tomb.

If the God of the universe has revealed himself in and to his creation, then nothing could be more important than responding to God's continuing initiatives, that is, by acknowledging his creation, obeying his laws, and receiving his redemption. God's coming in the Christ event is modeled in the Hebrew story of Jacob's ladder where the messenger came "down" to Jacob rather than Jacob going "up" to God.

PRIDE AND ACCOUNTABILITY

Human pride, however, tries to reverse God's initiatives. With a devious inversion, the creature seizes the initiative and tries to dictate the terms of belief and unbelief. We try to account for the creation of the universe without reference to the Creator. We try to administer governments and legal systems without reference to the divine lawgiver. And we write off the Christ event as a humanistic illusion.

Moses Maimonides (1135–1204), one of the truly great Jewish scholars, showed profound insight when he explained that there are two forms of idolatry: The first form involves worshiping strange gods or substituting some created god-form in place of the uncreated reality of God. "The second form of idolatry, however, is a good deal more subtle than the pagan form of idolatry, and is a constant temptation even to the adherents of monotheistic religions. For this form of idolatry does not err in the object of its worship but rather, it errs in worshiping this true God in a way inconsistent with what little we know about God and his interest in the world."[1]

Modern/postmodern people fit Maimonides' second definition perfectly. Even when we acknowledge the existence of God, we seek to please or appease God with a self-help mentality. Instead of honoring God, we honor ourselves with the things we build with our hands and the ideas we create with our minds. Vainglory is substituted for the glory of God, and, in the end, the glorification of "self" becomes a perverse echo of God's glory.

It is no accident that Western civilization became increasingly humanistic, as it passed from Christendom, to early modernity, and now to the late modern/postmodern era. We see it in the humanistic art of the Renaissance, in the Reformation's emphasis on the individual, in the self-interest of capitalism, and in Marxism's theory that individuals are shaped by class conflict. The growing secularization isolated and then insulated the "individual" from his or her relationship with God. Instead of identifying the dignity of the individual as having been created in the image of God, humanistic "rights" were increasingly associated with political science, economics, and avant-garde social ideas.

The Declaration of Independence (1776) says, "We hold these truths to be self-evident, that all men are created equal, that they are *endowed by their Creator with certain unalienable Rights,* that among these are Life, Liberty, and the pursuit of Happiness." People still cling to the idea of unalienable rights, but many have abandoned the idea "that they are endowed by their Creator."

Humanistic ideas are increasingly understood as the sole justifications for "human rights," and political action has led national governments and international organizations to codify various "rights." For example, the organization of the United Nations (UN) after World War II led to the UN's Universal Declaration of Human Rights where Article 1 says,

---

1. Novak, "The Mind of Maimonides," 30.

Christianity and the Outsider

"All human beings are born free and equal in dignity and rights. They are endowed with reason and conscience and should act towards one another in a spirit of brotherhood." Notably, instead of rights being "endowed by their Creator" they are "endowed with reason and conscience."

In other words, the humanistic rationale has been used to politicize the idea of God-given "rights" to include all kinds of socio-political issues including the rights of defendants in criminal cases, the civil rights of minorities, women's rights, abortion rights, children's rights, gay rights, and on and on. The rights trend has now been extended to "animal rights." Obviously, turkeys cannot avoid the Thanksgiving dinner table by asserting their own "rights." Therefore, animal rights advocates take an "I am my brother's keeper" approach in defending the "rights" of poultry, cattle, and other animals on the food chain. In the end, the human dignity of having been created in the image of God is reduced to a materialistic naturalism where no distinction is made between human beings and the beasts of the field.

My point is not to belittle the various rights issues and the socio-political ideas that I have often defended in the courtroom. What I am saying is that the human dignity with which we are "endowed" is the result of our having been created in the image of God as opposed to a state of mind that says social, political, or economic "rights" are a matter of human autonomy.

Unfortunately, some of the positive ideas that we associate with modern science and the individualistic ideals of democracy and capitalism can also feed human pride. As mentioned earlier, Richard Dawkins put human pride in the spotlight when he said, "An atheist in this sense of philosophical naturalist is somebody who believes there is nothing beyond the natural, physical world, no supernatural creative intelligence lurking behind the observable universe, no soul that outlasts the body and no miracles—except in the sense of natural phenomena that we don't yet understand."[2] Human braggadocio regarding creaturely prowess is like a frightened child whistling in the dark.

The ultimate form of human dignity is that God has revealed himself to humanity and that each individual is personally accountable to him. Indeed, I would argue that all the posturing in the world does not abrogate our accountability to God. We are born as individuals, we die as

---

2. Dawkins, *The God Delusion*, 13–14.

individuals, and we will face God as individuals. This is the ultimate form of individuality.

The Christian doctrine of revelation has always been troubling because it says God holds Christians and non-Christians equally accountable for sin. The question has always been: How can the gospel hold people accountable when they have never heard the gospel message? What does Christianity say about the African mother or father who died before the Christian missionary brought the gospel message to the son? These questions raise the issue of Christianity's relationship with secularism and other world religions, and they demand an honest response.

ACCOUNTABILITY PLUS REMEDY

The response begins by calling attention to the fact that the Judeo-Christian revelation has two sides just as a coin has heads and tails. On one side there is human accountability *for* sin, and on the other side there is divine remedy *from* sin.

The idea of general accountability for sin would seem to imply the existence of a general remedy, that is, a remedy that would be equally available to all people whether they lived before or after the Christ event and whether they lived inside or outside the Judeo-Christian covenants.

The problem is that in the first few chapters of Romans, the apostle Paul gives a detailed explanation regarding general accountability *without providing a rationale for a general remedy*. In chapter 1, for example, he hints at the idea of a general remedy when he says, "that which is known about God is evident within them" and then says God's "eternal power and divine nature have been clearly seen, being understood through what has been made so that they are without excuse" (Rom 1:19–20). Notice, however, that this aspect of general revelation is limited to the question of accountability. Rather than suggesting a general remedy from sin, Paul says the general understanding means "they are without excuse."

Paul's association with general revelation as remedy is similar to what lawyers and judges call *obiter dictum*, literally, "something said in passing." In a court's decision, *dictum* refers to something in the court's opinion that is incidental to the case in chief. Legally, the *dictum* is not required in order for the court to render its decision. Sometimes a written opinion alludes to some point without making it part of the binding precedent for future cases. The comment may have been an aside and not critical to the issue before the court; the case may not have presented enough information to allow a definitive exposition; or the court may have deferred the matter to another time and place. Sometimes the court will simply postpone the exposition of an issue so that it can be dealt with more definitively in a different context. For whatever reason, the *dictum* is mentioned in passing, but it is not fully explained at that point in time.

I am suggesting that in the first two and a half chapters of Romans, the apostle Paul established general revelation in relationship to humanity's general accountability *for sin*, but he did not present general revelation in the context of a general remedy *from sin*. The argument that all people are accountable to God and that the knowledge of God "is evident within" us would seem to imply an equivalence between accountability and remedy. However, having nailed down the argument regarding general accountability in Rom 3:19–20, Paul moved on without dealing with the idea of a general remedy. Indeed, his reticence regarding the possibility of a general remedy stands in sharp contrast to his extended discussion of the special remedy that begins with Rom 3:21.

Special revelation acknowledges that God created the heavens and the earth, including time and space—Therefore, he is outside historical time and space. However, "in the fullness of time," he intervened in history in the person of Jesus Christ (Gal 4:4). Paul's argument for special revelation is a carefully reasoned polemic that identifies Jesus of Nazareth as both Jewish Messiah and the risen Christ of the new covenant. In fact, Paul viewed his ministry as a divine calling to extend God's special revelation to the non-Jewish world.

As the fourth gospel says, Jesus was and is the eternal "Word" of God physically manifested on earth—"In the beginning was the *Word* and the Word was with God, and the Word was God . . . And the *Word became flesh* and dwelt among us, and we beheld His glory, glory as of the only begotten from the Father, full of grace and truth . . . He who has seen Me has seen the Father . . . " (John 1:1,14, 14:9).

The Judeo-Christian tradition has a "high view" of Scripture which says the God of heaven not only revealed himself in the person of Jesus Christ, but also caused the record of his revelation to be set forth in the Bible—"These things I have written to you who believe in the name of the Son of God, in order that you may know that you have eternal life" (1 John 5:13).

Revelation as Christ Event: Divine Redemption

Those who have a "low view" of Scripture contend that the Bible is like any other book written by men. For example, the early modern works of Spinoza (1632–1677) and David Hume (1711–1776) presuppose a naturalistic interpretation of all things religious. More recently, the "Jesus Seminar" project, which is made up of over one hundred liberal scholars, has further popularized non-traditional views. They say Jesus was mortal like any other individual, he was not resurrected from the dead, and there were no miracles. Most liberal scholars, including the Jesus Seminar, rely on human reason, and their criticism of biblical texts is based on humanistic presuppositions. However, to insist on humanistic limitations in a spiritual discussion is like a man trying to lift himself by pulling on his own bootstraps.

Textual criticism can also be leveled against the writings of other world religions as well as the writings of philosophers like Plato and Aristotle and historians like Herodotus and Thucydides. But these non-biblical writings are often accorded more dignity and respect than the Bible. I have always found it amazing that skeptics and critics are quick to denigrate the biblical record, but they tend to accept other ancient manuscripts at face value.

Unfortunately, skeptics ignore the extraordinary nature of the biblical record. The Bible is not one book but sixty-six books written over many years by forty different people from many different cultures, nationalities, and walks of life. Yet it contains an integrated story that has been shown to be truthful and helpful to all kinds of people in all kinds of situations. Moreover, it contains numerous prophecies regarding the promised Messiah, many of which have already been fulfilled.

The Messianic promises were introduced in the Old Testament, especially in the Psalms and by the prophets, and then reaffirmed in the New Testament. Both of these traditions claim to have a covenant relationship with God, and both look forward to a Messianic future. Christian Scripture goes on to declare that Isaiah's prophecy of "God with us" was Christ's first advent, and that we must continue to look forward to his "second coming" as a second advent.

Jewish and Christian perspectives differ regarding the nature of the Messianic event, but the underlying commonality is that both traditions point unequivocally to special revelation as a divine phenomenon. On one side of the Christ event, Hebrew Scripture speaks of God's covenant with Israel and looks forward to a divine advent in the Messianic future.

On the other side, Christian Scripture affirms God's "covenant" with Israel as well as the "new covenant" that identifies Jesus of Nazareth as Israel's Messiah. As Isaiah predicted, he was "despised and forsaken of men, A man of sorrows and acquainted with grief... But he was pierced through for our transgressions [and] the Lord has caused the iniquity of us all To fall on Him... Because He poured out Himself to death, And been numbered with the transgressors" (Isa 53:3, 5–6, 12).

Special revelation, as set forth in the Christian tradition, says God intervened in human history as a once-for-all-time manifestation of himself in the person of Jesus Christ—fully God and fully man. The uniqueness of the Christ event is revealed in the resurrected Christ and embodied in the continuing message of the church.

During Jesus' earthly ministry, the scribes and Pharisees said, "Teacher, we want to see a sign," (that is, a sign of God's special revelation), but Jesus said, "An evil and adulterous generation craves for a sign; and yet no sign shall be given to it but the sign of Jonah the prophet; for just as Jonah was three days and three nights in the belly of the sea monster, so shall the Son of Man be three days and three nights in the heart of the earth" (Matt 12:38–40).

Things haven't changed much. First century critics wanted practical evidence, and contemporary critics are obsessed with the empirical evidence of natural science. But Jesus said his death-burial-resurrection *was* the "sign." Jesus is the light of the world, and special revelation is like a fiber-optic that carries that light throughout the Bible and into the world.

Special revelation stands in sharp contrast to general revelation. Whereas special revelation is understood in the context of God's unique relationships with Israel and Christianity, general revelation is usually understood as the impact God has on the rest of humanity as seen in nature, history, or conscience.

The difference between special and general revelation is especially pronounced when it comes to the doctrine of salvation. Theological conservatives say general revelation is not salvific because salvation requires the individual to have conscious faith in Jesus Christ and his atonement. Theological liberals, on the other hand, have abandoned the traditional view that salvation is based upon Christ's atonement and adopted the popular notion that "many roads" lead to God. In spite of the traditional differences, there are people in both camps who have struggled with the

Revelation as Christ Event: Divine Redemption

enigma that general revelation seems to provide enough knowledge to condemn the sinner but not enough to redeem him.

The "good news" of Christ's atonement is the foundation of special revelation and the central theme in the life and work of the apostle Paul (1Cor 3:10–11). Yet, as mentioned earlier, Paul seems to have treated accountability and remedy rather differently. He discussed "accountability" in terms of general revelation, but "remedy" was focused on special revelation.

If Paul explained our *accountability* in terms of general revelation where *all* people are equally accountable to God, but limited the *remedy* to special revelation, it could mean that the full extent of Christ's role in general revelation was beyond the reach of Paul's era. However, this silence regarding a "general remedy" should not come as a surprise to Bible students. As mentioned earlier, the apostle acknowledged his own limitations when he said, "Oh, the depth . . . of God! How unsearchable are His judgments and unfathomable His ways! For who has known the mind of the Lord, or who became His counselor" (Rom 11:33–34)?

Job set the tone for humanity's limited understanding of the things of God when he said, "I know that Thou canst do all things, And that no purpose of Thine can be thwarted. Who is this that hides counsel without knowledge? Therefore I have declared that which I did not understand, Things too wonderful for me, which I did not know . . . Therefore I retract, And *I repent* in dust and ashes" (Job 42:2–3, 6).

Even Jesus indicated that greater things would unfold in the future— "Truly, truly, I say to you, he who believes in Me, the works that I do shall he do also; and *greater* works than these shall he do, because I go to the Father" (John 14:12).

The Bible is unequivocal regarding revelation when it deals with humanity's *general accountability* for sin, but it is mostly silent regarding a *general remedy* from sin. Why does the Bible mandate general accountability *for* sin but seem to provide a limited remedy *from* sin? In other words, does the traditional view present a partial picture of revelation?

7

Revelation: Looking Back

Accountability and remedy are different aspects of revelation, but they are related to each other like entering and leaving a tunnel. The law requires accountability for sin like entering the darkness of a tunnel. However, the Christ event provides a remedy from sin like emerging into the light of day. What is general and special revelation, and what is the difference? And why does liberal theology minimize the impact of special revelation, while conservative theology minimizes the scope of general revelation?

ACCOUNTABILITY AND REMEDY

The apostle Paul began the Book of Romans with a discussion of general revelation in order to establish that "there is no partiality with God" (Rom 2:11). He spent most of the first three chapters of Romans developing a meticulous argument confirming that *all* human beings have general accountability for sin (Rom 1:1—3:20). He summed up the general indictment with a statement that says, ". . . Jews and Greeks [non-Jews] are *all* under sin; as it is written, There is none righteous, not even one; There is none who understands, There is none who seeks for God; *All* have turned aside, together they have become useless; There is none who does good, There is not even one" (Rom 3:9–12).

Paul began with humanity's general accountability *for sin*, but he did not provide a corresponding discussion of a general remedy *from sin*. Instead, he went directly into a discussion of special revelation and the special remedy that had become available through Christ and his new covenant.

Beginning with Rom 3:21 and continuing throughout Romans and all of Paul's other epistles, he repeatedly made the connection between general accountability and the special remedy that had been made available to those who are privy to the new covenant. But he never gave a detailed explanation regarding a possible connection between the "general accountability" of all people and a "general remedy" that might be available to all people. Indeed, there is no exposition regarding either the existence or nonexistence of a general remedy.

In view of Paul's extended discussion of general accountability, it would have been logical for him to discuss the existence or nonexistence of a general remedy, but he didn't expand the idea of general accountability to include a general remedy. As previously mentioned, general remedy is like the *obiter dictum* of an appellate judge where "something is said in passing," but it is not made the central issue in the case.

Paul's initial objective in the Book of Romans was to establish humanity's general accountability to God, and he was unequivocal in accomplishing that task. In chapter 1 of Romans he said:

> . . . that which is known about God is evident within them; for God made it evident to them. For since the creation of the world His invisible attributes, His eternal power and divine nature, have been clearly seen, being understood through what has been made, so that they are without excuse. For even though they knew God, they did not honor Him as God, or give thanks; but they became futile in their speculations, and their foolish heart was darkened. Professing to be wise, they became fools, and exchanged the glory of the incorruptible God for an image in the form of corruptible man and of birds and four-footed animals and crawling creatures (Rom 1:19–23).

The apostle alluded to the possibility of a general remedy in a few places and maybe even foreshadowed the issue in his missionary work in

Lystra and Athens, but he did not extend his discussion of general revelation to include the idea of a general remedy from sin.

Matthew supported the possibility of general revelation with the words of Jesus, who said, "But I say to you, love your enemies, and pray for those who persecute you in order that you may be sons of your Father who is in heaven; *for He causes His sun to rise on the evil and the good, and sends rain on the righteous and the unrighteous*" (Matt 5:44–45).

The New Testament writers even had Old Testament precedent for the idea of general revelation. King David summed up the situation when he said:

> The heavens are telling of the glory of God;
> And their expanse is declaring the work of His hands.
> Day to day pours forth speech,
> And night to night reveals knowledge.
> There is no speech, nor are there words;
> Their voice is not heard.
> Their line has gone out through all the earth,
> And their utterances to the end of the world (Ps 19:1–4).

General revelation is obvious with reference to creation and humanity's general accountability for sin. However, the Christ event shifted the focus from general revelation to special revelation.

THE MYSTERY OF GENERAL REVELATION

The truth is that general revelation is as shrouded in mystery today as it was two thousand years ago, and the writings of the apostle Paul are part of the continuing mystery. That is, Paul was unequivocal regarding humanity's general accountability *for sin*, but the possibility of a general remedy *from sin* is still controversial.

Some people "solve" the general remedy dilemma by simply denying the existence of general revelation except as it relates to creation and the moral law. However, denial is a curious position for the new covenant insider who says *all* people are equally accountable for sin but that God's remedy from sin is limited to the insiders who enjoy the benefits of the new covenant. Insiders minimize the significance of general revelation and dismiss the idea of a general remedy from sin.

Revelation: Looking Back

Others contend that accountability for sin is inconsistent with the idea of a loving God. Therefore, they advocate some form of Universalism where the general revelation of a loving God allegedly makes eternal life available to all people. They assume the existence of a general remedy from sin based upon the splendor of creation and the grace of a loving God. Universalism minimizes the significance of special revelation and ignores the atonement of Jesus Christ.

Still others engage in pure speculation. Disregarding the Judeo-Christian tradition, they simply strike out on their own, inventing new spiritualities along the way. The new religious pluralism encourages the individual autonomy of people like Sheila, the young woman in *Habits of the Heart* who said: " I believe in God. I'm not a religious fanatic. I can't remember the last time I went to church. My faith has carried me a long way. It's Sheilaism. Just my own little voice."[1]

The modern mentality caters to the radical autonomy of the individual and creates a comfort zone for the delusional idea of inventing one's own idea of ultimate reality. Indeed, the alleged autonomy of the individual is the same whether understood as the scholarly undertaking of a philosopher like Frederick Nietzsche, a scientific undertaking like the New Atheism of Richard Dawkins, or the casual observations of an average person like Sheila and her "Sheilaism."

Personal speculation is much like writing fantasy or science fiction. In fact, some forms of science fiction have morphed into "religions" like the Scientology movement and the tiny Heaven's Gate sect that ended with the group suicides that occurred in 1997.

Unfortunately, today's religious pluralism assumes spiritual equivalence among the various spiritualities, and Christianity is treated like any other philosophy or religion.

MODERN CREDIBILITY

Of course, the ultimate question is whether the gospel account has credibility in a modern/postmodern world—That is, is divine forgiveness necessary, and is it available only through Jesus Christ?

Most Christian accounts of general revelation are problematic. Liberals explain general revelation as a redemptive phenomenon separate

---

1. Bellah et al., *Habits of the Heart*, 221.

Christianity and the Outsider

and apart from the Christ event, thereby diminishing the significance of Christ. Conservatives, on the other hand, minimize the significance of general revelation by contending that general revelation leads one to find and follow Christ, turning "general" revelation into an expanded version of special revelation.

Whether conservative or liberal, most theologians are caught up in the duality of an either/or argument. Forced onto one side of the equation or the other, they view salvation as either the *exclusive* domain of special revelation or as the *inclusive* domain of general revelation:

On one side, theologians identify Jesus Christ as God's special revelation to the absolute *exclusion* of the outsiders who are strangers to the new covenant. Some even exclude those who disagree with their interpretation of Holy Writ. Reformation history reveals that in 1527, Roman Catholic authorities tried and executed Rev. Felix Manz for re-baptizing Protestant converts. Perhaps the worse case scenario is the story of Michael Servetus (1511–1553) who avoided prosecution for heresy by escaping from the Catholics. He then made his way to Protestant Geneva, where Protestant authorities later burned him at the stake as a non-Trinitarian heretic. Of course, such extremism is no longer acceptable, but some well-meaning Christian leaders still engage in the practice of excluding those who disagree with their interpretation of the Scripture. They adhere to a Christology that says Jesus is "God with us," but they have become so attached to their own tradition that they try to limit God and lose the freshness of the Spirit.

Perhaps Calvin College professor James K.A. Smith got it right when he said God can still surprise people. In a *Christianity Today* article entitled "Teaching a Calvinist to Dance," Smith said:

> The theological giants of the Reformed tradition—Calvin, Edwards, Kuyper, and others—have put God's sovereignty at the center and heart of a Reformed 'world – and life-view.' God is the Lord of the cosmos; God is free from having to meet our expectations; God is sovereign in his election of the people of God. I think there is an interesting way in which Pentecostals live out a spirituality that takes that sovereignty really, really seriously. In particular, I think Pentecostal spirituality and charismatic worship take the sovereignty of God so seriously that you might actually be *surprised* by God every once in a while. You are open and expectant that the Spirit of God is sometimes going to surprise you,

because God is free to act in ways that might differ from *your* set of expectations.[2]

On the other side, some *inclusive* theologians acknowledge the Christ event, but they have acquiesced to modernity in a way that has compromised the gospel of Jesus Christ. In this modern scenario, God has supposedly revealed himself to humanity—but he did so without reference to a divinely inspired Bible, without reference to the atonement of Jesus Christ, and without reference to an understanding of the church as the "bride of Christ." Jesus is perceived as a great soul and a wonderful teacher, but he is believed to have been a human being like any other human being. Having disclaimed the metaphysical nature of the Christ event, the modern/postmodern mentality subscribes to the idea that God's general revelation is found in nature, in human consciousness, or in some other temporal medium.

In other words, conservative church leaders focus on special revelation and neglect or exclude general revelation. They see their entree as the only item on an a la carte menu. Meanwhile, liberal church leaders focus on general revelation and neglect or exclude special revelation. They view Christianity as one of many items on a spiritual smorgasbord. Maybe a reevaluation of revelation will whet spiritual appetites on both sides of the theological divide.

---

2. Smith, J.K. "Teaching A Calvinist to Dance," para. 1.

Part III
The Case for the Constant Christ

The Constant Christ

8

Revelation: A New Perspective

Many people are tired of the uncertainty and the incivility that are rampant in today's secular world. They are looking for a new rationale, a rationale that will reaffirm the spirit of Robert Browning's famous poem that says, "God's in his heaven, All's right with the world."

HISTORICAL TRANSITION

The physics of Copernicus (1473–1543) and Galileo (1564–1642) turned science and theology upside down in the seventeenth century. Is it possible that the physics of Albert Einstein (1879–1955) that turned the scientific world upside down in the twentieth century might turn the theological world upside down in the twenty-first century? God is God— He never changes! But when our conception of the world changes, we are obliged to reexamine our understanding of that world as well as our finite perception of its infinite Creator.

Historically, the new physics would not be the first time scientific changes regarding the temporal world have influenced the biblical worldview. Probably, the most dramatic transition has been in cosmology where science has shifted from the earth being the center of the universe, to the sun being the center of the universe, to the present scenario where our whole galaxy is a tiny part of an expanding universe. The latest phase in the historical process is the transition from the classical physics of Isaac Newton (1642–1727) to the new physics of Einstein and many others. The new model of understanding is built around the theory of relativity. (See Appendix Sec. 3.00)

Admittedly, the theory of relativity with its moving frame of reference, uniform/non-uniform motion, and constant speed of light (the "c" in $E=mc^2$) is scientific. However, the relativity model has spiritual implications that might support a new rationale for the troubled world in which we live. That is, we live in a physical world that has a moving frame of reference that sometimes resembles the moving, changing uncertainty of human existence. (See Appendix Sec. 4.00)

However, the Bible says Jesus intervened in that troubled world with a view of bringing light out of darkness. Indeed, he said, "I am the *light of the world*" (John 8:12). The fact that the "constant" speed of light permeates the universe is analogous to the constant Christ who created and sustains that universe (John 1:1–5). Maybe his self-portrayal as the light of the world should be associated with the nature of light, itself, as well as the traditional idea of spiritual illumination.

If one understands the scientific fact that uniform motion and non-uniform motion are the two basic classifications in the theory of relativity, then he or she can more easily accept the theological fact that humanity's finite uniformity and God's infinite non-uniformity are the ultimate classifications in the doctrine of revelation. (See Appendix Sec. 5.00)

Similarly, if one understands the scientific fact that the "constant speed of light" in $E=mc^2$ is the connection between uniform motion and non-uniform motion, then he or she can more easily accept the theological fact that the "constant Christ" who is "the same yesterday and today, yes and forever" (Heb 13:8) is the ultimate connection between human uniformity and divine non-uniformity. (See Appendix Sec. 6.00)

One of the barriers to understanding the philosophical implications of relativity is that many people think relativity and relativism mean the same thing. Therefore, I have coined a new term to distinguish between these two worldviews:

Relativitism is the term I have used to show the inherent difference between relativity and relativism. Relativitism is unique because it is value-based—That is, it is based on the existence of *constant value* as manifested in the constant speed of light. The new term is necessary because after a hundred years, most people, including knowledgeable scholars, continue to discuss relativity and relativism as if they are the same. It is true that relativity is a scientific theory that features a *"moving frame of reference"* where everything in the universe is moving. However, those moving parts are "relative to" the constant speed of light. Therefore, "constant value" is the decisive component in the theory of relativity.

Relativism, on the other hand, has *no constant value*; therefore, it has *no frame of reference*. The misunderstanding occurs because relativism denies the existence of God and eternal values and is left with only the temporal world and its changing circumstances. The relativist is then forced to accept modern relativism where moral and ethical values allegedly change from time to time and place to place. It is appropriate, therefore, to describe relativity as having a *"moving* frame of reference" and relativism as having *"no* frame of reference." In other words, relativitism is a philosophy that reaffirms the existence of constant value, and relativism is a philosophy that has no constant value.

Judaism, Christianity, and most other religions utilize constant or eternal values as well as uniformity and non-uniformity in their theology without ever thinking about the theory of relativity. That is, they teach that human beings are part of a temporal world (our ultimate uniformity) and that this temporal world is somehow related to an eternal world (God's ultimate *non-uniformity*). Common sense would suggest the need for some form of communication between these two worlds such as a mediator who could speak the finite language of human experience as well as the infinite language of eternal values.

Traditional Christianity identifies Jesus Christ as that ultimate mediator between God and humanity. The essence of the gospel story is that the uniformity of humankind is related to the non-uniformity of God through the mediation of Jesus Christ. For example, the fourth gospel identifies Jesus as the communicating or mediating "Word" *(logos)* between God and humanity—"In the beginning was the Word and the Word was with God and the Word was God . . . And the *Word became flesh and dwelt among us, and we beheld His glory . . .* " (John 1:1, 14).

Perhaps the strongest biblical statement regarding God's intervention in human history in the person of Jesus Christ appears in chapter 2 of Philippians, where the apostle Paul did some human relations coaching with the Christians at Philippi. He said, "Do nothing from selfishness or empty conceit, but with humility of mind let each of you regard one

Christianity and the Outsider

another as more important than himself; do not merely look out for your own personal interests, but also for the interests of others" (Phil 2:3–4).

The apostle then explained *how* the Philippians could follow his instructions. They were to follow the example of Jesus—and what an example it is! The apostle said Jesus "existed in the form of God," but he did not cling to his "equality with God" as an honorary position. In other words, he did not hang onto his divine preeminence like a man might cling to his seat if he were about to be thrown from an airplane without a parachute. Instead, Christ voluntarily "emptied Himself, taking the form of a bond-servant, and being made in the likeness of men. And being found in appearance as a man, He humbled Himself by becoming obedient to the point of death, even death on a cross" (Phil 2:5–8).

Paul pointed out the uniqueness of Christ's sacrifice in chapter 5 of Romans when he said, "For one will hardly die for a righteous man; though perhaps for the good man someone would dare even to die. But God demonstrates His love toward us, in that while we were yet sinners, Christ died for *the ungodly*" (Rom 5:6–8). Dying for a relative, a friend, or some other good person is commendable, but dying for the ungodly people of the world is an extraordinary kind of sacrifice.

If Christ "died for the ungodly," then he must have died for the ungodly people who lived before him as well as for those who would live after him. Furthermore, if the Christ event reaches out in time and space, then any discussion of Christ as divine revelation should consider the impact of his sacrifice not only on covenant insiders (before and after the cross) but also on *non*-covenant outsiders (before and after the cross.)

Revelation, of course, is a subject that is burdened with traditions and controversies that go back thousands of years. Is it possible, therefore, for twenty-first-century Christianity to say anything new about God having revealed himself to his creation? And, if so, how should we begin a new discussion of an old subject? We can never forget the differences that separate Jews and Christians, but we should not ignore the mutuality that says *all* people are ultimately accountable to God, and that only God can provide mediation between himself and his creation. In spite of the obvious differences, Jews and Christians occupy some common ground, so maybe that commonality can serve as a platform to launch this new conversation.

God's "covenant with Israel" has been unfolding for almost four thousand years—From Abraham, to Moses, to David, to the prophets, to Titus's destruction of Jerusalem in 70 CE, through the Diaspora, to the Holocaust, to the reconstitution of Israel in 1948, to the present day. Judaism has never been the same since Titus destroyed the temple and the sacrificial system was lost, but it has now persevered for another two thousand years. We know the Jewish covenant is a continuing phenomenon because it has survived unspeakable hardships and because the Bible says it is "irrevocable" (Rom 11:29).

Christianity, also referred to as "the new covenant," has now been around for two thousand years, and, like the initial covenant with Israel, this new covenant has experienced difficult times. Believers have been persecuted throughout the life of the church. The church has overcome many challenges, including East-West schism, the trauma of the Protestant Reformation, and the continuing division of Protestantism into multiple denominations. Like the earlier covenant, the new covenant maintains that people are accountable to God for the way they live their lives.

Unfortunately, many in the modern/postmodern West, including some who attend churches and synagogues, have simply rejected the idea of revelation, including the idea that human beings are accountable to God. If they have any concept of spirituality at all, it is that human consciousness is part of a transcendent whole. They see themselves as a part of a God-like spirit or "force"—like a spark is part of a fire or a drop of water is part of the ocean. They try to eliminate the idea of personal accountability to God by theorizing that they themselves are part of God's transcendence and that all people have a common destiny. Many of them reject the Judeo-Christian revelation, but they cling to the moral teachings of Judaism or Christianity.

THE HISTORICAL WAVES

I have borrowed the "wave" metaphor from Alvin Toffler's book *The Third Wave* in which he divided civilization into the agricultural wave, the industrial wave, and the information wave. In a similar way, I am suggesting that Western civilization has unfolded as a series of historical "waves" that reflect the transition from the premodern era, to the modern/postmodern era, to whatever is coming next. Of course, as Toffler pointed out, these "grand metaphors" allow one to organize vast amounts of information, but they are limited in their ability to provide detailed coverage of specific situations.[1]

Anyone who has ever been to the beach knows that a wave hits the beach at one spot and then ripples down the coastline hitting successive spots at later times. For example, one society may be experiencing the first wave, while another society has gone on to modernity's second wave. Similarly, the second wave may have run its course in another society, and it may be experiencing the uncertainty of not knowing what is coming next.

My study uses the wave metaphor to suggest the existence of a historical panorama where philosophical and theological "waves" are identified as set forth in the following graphic:

FIRST WAVE:	SECOND WAVE:	THIRD WAVE:
Premodern era	Modern/postmodern era	Next era
Ancient regimes	Enlightenment movement	Next "movement"
Aristocratic control	Bourgeois control	Autonomous factions
Upper class emphasis	Middle class emphasis	Egalitarian emphasis
Theological focus	Scientific focus	Interdisciplinary focus
Objective mode	Subjective mode	Relativity mode
Absolutism	Relativism	Relativitism
Fixed frame of reference	No frame of reference	Moving frame of reference
Magna Carta 1215	American Declaration of Independence 1776	Universal Declaration of Human Rights 1948
	Declaration of the Rights of Man 1789	

PREMODERN PERSPECTIVE: THE FIRST WAVE

The first wave represents the premodern era where classical and medieval scholars relied upon the old absolutes, the idea of a fixed frame, and a primal sense of unity. They used the idea of hierarchy to reach the oneness and sameness of an ideal world. Particulars were at the bottom of the hierarchy, and generalizations were up above. For example, "dog" is particular, whereas "animal" is general; "don't hurt Mary" is particular, but "be kind to one another" is general; "don't steal my coat" is particular, while "thou shall not steal" is general. (See Appendix Sec. 8.00)

---

1. Toffler, *The Third Wave*, 4–6.

With traditional classifications, the universals are at the top of the ladder. The nature of the classification hierarchy can be seen in the description of my son's dog from "Scout," to Labrador, to canine, to mammal. There is diversity within hierarchy, but diversity always looks up the ladder—to the oneness or sameness of a *"higher* uniformity." Understandably, kings were at the top of the political hierarchy in the premodern era, just as God was the top of the spiritual hierarchy.

MODERN/POSTMODERN PERSPECTIVE: THE SECOND WAVE

The second wave began with the modern era. However, modernity has been so pervasive that it has to be further divided into early modern, late modern and postmodern categories: (See Appendix Sec. 9.00)

Early Modern Era

Early modern thinkers like Rene Descartes (1596–1650), John Locke (1632–1704), Jean Jacques Rousseau (1712–1778), Immanuel Kant (1724–1804), and Georg Hegel (1770–1831) show the transition from medieval times to the modern era. However, each of their philosophical systems led to an ultimate unity. Each one tried to identify the errors of the past and to establish a baseline upon which future generations could rely. They produced a series of grand systems or "uniformities," but each one was eventually determined to be inadequate. Each of the early modern philosophers tried to draw an inclusive circle that would provide a comprehensive philosophy regarding human existence, but the passage of time always produced differences or "non-uniformities" that were outside the grand circle. Over the years, new theories added missing pieces to the puzzle, but they all fell short of the ideal. (See Appendix Sec. 9.10)

Adding the idea of *time*, Hegel developed one of the last attempts to create an all-inclusive system. The Hegelian dialectical method of argument leaned toward oneness or sameness because it presupposed the existence of a "dialectical method" that was hardwired, so to speak, to the divine. With Hegel's spiritual dialectic, the sameness of uniformity (thesis) and the difference or negation of non-uniformity (antithesis) were understood to be part of an eternal process that would always evolve into the "*next* uniformity" (synthesis). Hegel claimed that his process of thesis, antithesis, and synthesis would continue indefinitely.

Hegel's idea of an evolving process has been adapted in various ways to evolutionary science, process theology, as well as other forms of process that unfold over time. Perhaps most notably, Karl Marx transformed Hegel's "dialectical method" into "dialectical materialism" where atheistic Communism was to be history's final synthesis.

Whereas premodern hierarchies had a spatial connotation that looked *upward* to God, the modern dialectic has a humanistic connotation. It is an evolving process that looks either *inward* to the subjectivity of the human mind or *forward* to a humanistic future. On one hand, the old idea of hierarchy would allegedly culminate in a theology of divine perfection; on the other hand, the modern dialectic was supposed to culminate in human perfection.

Ironically, some of the earlier thought patterns are now being reinvented as new spiritual movements. For example, New Age mysticism looks forward to the so-called "Age of Aquarius" where holistic ideals are supposed to bring enlightenment and a better world. Psychotherapy and various other forms of psychology look inward for fulfillment and solutions to life's problems. Other ideologies, including Scientology and neo-Marxism, look forward to training and processing that will allegedly bring a better future. Some seek a *higher* uniformity, while others are looking for the *next* uniformity.

The historical fact is that both the old hierarchies and the modern dialectic obscure the primal contrast between sameness and difference—especially the great gulf between the uniformity of humankind and the non-uniformity of God.

Late Modern Era

Late modern thinkers like Friedrich Nietzsche (1844–1900), Sigmund Freud (1856–1939), Ferdinand De Saussure (1857–1913), and Martin Heidegger (1889–1976) put the spotlight on difference, especially the *contrast* between sameness and difference. (See Appendix Sec. 9.20)

These late modern writers used "difference . . . to express a sense of meaning emerging from some radical otherness rather than progressing from a primal unity . . ." (Detweiler 14). They realized that the premodern

Revelation: A New Perspective

oneness of hierarchy and the modern oneness of synthesis are both flawed because "difference" always arrives to challenge the unity of "sameness," just as "other" always arrives to challenge the oneness of "self."

Postmodern Era

The late modern idea of difference is *not "different enough"* for the so-called postmodern thinkers who have now arrived on the scene. They object to the earlier idea of difference because they realize that it, too, "... always at last comes under the sovereignty of a basic oneness."[2] In other words, even with the late modern idea of difference, human experience is erroneously brought under a single umbrella. (See Appendix Sec. 9.30)

Jacques Derrida (1930–2004), one of the most prominent postmodern thinkers, was convinced that the radical other was not radical enough. You might say he *radicalized the radical other*. For Derrida, traditional meaning and religious certainty are misguided ideals. Part of his strategy was to coin new words and to invent new meanings for old words. His new vocabulary was then used to facilitate a new discussion of "otherness."

Under Derrida's coinage, the difference of the *radical other* in the late modern perspective becomes the "diffe*r*ance" of a *more radical other* in the postmodern perspective. For example, the French word *"difference"* trades on *"differre"* from Latin and *"differer"* from French. Derrida used this double entendre to coin the word "diffe*r*ance," giving it a twofold connotation: For Derrida, "diffe*r*ance" means both to differ (as in "to be other than") *and* to defer (as in "held off, eternally deferred"). His "diffe*r*ance" helped him redefine words like "trace" and "play" (as in a mere trace of the old and the play of the new) in order to create a tension that vouches for the gulf that exists between the uniformity of sameness and the non-uniformity of otherness.

Derrida argued for the existence of a radical differential that would discredit traditional ideas of meaning in philosophy and theology. He referred to this differential or "diffe*r*ance" as an unnamable tension, even as he tried to avoid the "suspicion that he was attempting to create an

---

2. Detweiler, "No Place to Start," 14.

alternate ontology, a countertheology, or even a disguised celebration of Being"[3]

Derrida said,

> This unnamable is not an ineffable Being, which no name could approach: God, for example. This unnamable is the play, which makes possible nominal effects, the *relatively* unitary and atomic structures that are called names ... What we know ... is that there has never been, never will be, a unique word, a master-name. This is why the thought of the letter *"a"* in differ*a*nce is not the primary prescription or the prophetic annunciation of an imminent and as yet unheard-of nomination. There is nothing kerygmatic about this 'word,' provided that one perceives its decapita(liza)tion.[4]

Leave it to a Frenchman to use "decapitation" in his attempt to finish off the old order! Trying to discredit the idea that Jesus Christ is the "unique word (or) master-name"—as in John 1:1 where "the Word was with God and the Word was God"—Derrida used his cutting wit not only to decapitalize "the word" linguistically, but also to "decapitate" the idea of a master-name.

Ironically, if Jesus had been French and executed in 1792, he would probably have been guillotined instead of crucified. In that scenario, Derrida would have been accidentally correct, just as Caiaphas was unwittingly truthful when he said, "it is expedient for you that one man should die for the people, and that the whole nation should not perish (John 11:50).

At least Derrida was intellectually honest. He argued that there is *no* mediating word between human uniformity and the non-uniformity of his unnamable "tension." Derrida pointed to the *"a"* in "differance" as a *"trace* of the meaning that never arrives."[5] Of course, this postmodern mentality flies in the face of the fourth gospel where Christ is identified as the "Word" of God—That is, "the Word was with God, and the Word was God ... And the Word became flesh and dwelt among us ... " (John 1:1, 14).

No one would characterize the early Derrida as spiritual much less religious. However, his use of the uniformity/non-uniformity model, or as

---

3. Ibid., 15.
4. Derrida, "Difference," 16.
5. Detweiler, "No Place to Start," 16.

he called it "bipolar opposition" (justice/injustice, self/other, male/female, etc.), is actually indicative of the gulf that exists between the uniformity of humankind and the non-uniformity of God.

In Derrida's later years, his work developed a new or at least a deeper connotation that has caused some writers to suggest that postmodern theories have serious implications for theology. Indeed, the ongoing struggle to provide an interface between postmodern philosophy and traditional theology can be seen in some unusual book titles coming from within the Christian tradition—to wit: *The Prayers and Tears of Jacques Derrida: Religion Without Religion* (1997) by John Caputo; *Who's Afraid of Postmodernism?: Taking Derrida, Lyotard, and Foucault to Church* (2006) by James K.A. Smith; *What Would Jesus Deconstruct?: The Good News of Postmodernism for the Church* (2007) by John Caputo and Brian McLaren; and *Religion With/Out Religion: The Prayers and Tears of John Caputo* (2008) Edited by James Olthuis.

Literary critic Terry Eagleton (1943-) is another postmodernist who has struggled with the idea of traditional meaning. He says:

> Meaning ... is rather a kind of constant flickering of presence and absence together. Reading a text is more like tracing this process of constant flickering than it is like counting the beads on a necklace. There is also another sense in which we can never quite close our fists over meaning, which arises from the fact that language is a temporal process. When I read a sentence, the meaning of it is always somehow suspended, something deferred or still to come ... earlier meanings are modified by later ones, and although the sentence may come to an end, the process of language itself does not ... I do not grasp the sense of the sentence just by mechanically piling one word on the other: for the words to compose some *relatively* coherent meaning at all, each one of them must, so to speak, contain the trace of the ones which have gone before, and hold itself open to the trace of those which are coming after.[6]

Eagleton is like a hunter who hits two birds with one shot when he says the reading of a text is more like a "constant flickering" than "counting the beads on a necklace." Counting the beads on a necklace is reminiscent of the old absolutism and the *linear* thinking that endorsed the use of rosary beads in religion. That same linear thinking produced the hierarchies that were used in the construction of grandiose systems of

---

6. Eagleton, *Literary Theory*, 128.

philosophy and theology. However, the "constant flickering" is *nonlinear* and indicative of the constant speed of light as it radiates into surrounding space or the constant Christ as his love spreads out in all directions.

The traditional idea of "fixed" hierarchies in philosophy and theology and Hegel's "fixed" dialectic (thesis, antithesis, and synthesis) were eventually discredited. However, the loss of these "fixed" frames of reference created a value vacuum, and modern/postmodern relativism flowed into the emptiness. In other words, the demise of the old *absolutism* opened the door to modern *relativism*.

In the absence of absolutism with its *fixed* frame of reference, late modern/postmodern thinkers have resorted to relativism where there is *no* frame of reference. Eagleton's suggestion that meaning "is always somehow suspended . . . a kind of constant flickering of presence and absence together"[7] is typical of late modern/postmodern subjectivity where the only constant is change, itself. Indeed, in the postmodern view of Derrida, meaning is "held off, eternally deferred."[8]

Drew University's Thomas Oden has described the postmodern mentality as "ultramodern" rather than "postmodern."[9] Oden's critique has been condensed into the "four fallen idols" that led to the demise of modernity, that is, autonomous individualism, narcissistic hedonism, reductive naturalism, and absolute moral relativism.[10] Is meaning "eternally" deferred or merely suspended and waiting for a new consensus to arrive—like the next wave to hit the beach?

THE NEW PERSPECTIVE: THE THIRD WAVE

I am reminded of Franz Kafka's suggestion that maybe there has been a "pause in history." Perhaps ideas must remain "up in the air" until philosophy and theology can catch up with the paradigm shift that has been transforming Western civilization over the last half-century or so.

I can't summarize the transition any better than I did in *The Gospel According to Relativity* when I said:

---

7. Ibid., 128.
8. Derrida, "Difference," 16.
9. Oden, *After Modernity . . . What?*, 77.
10. Erickson, *Postmodernizing the Faith*, 51–52.

Revelation: A New Perspective

Franz Kafka (1883–1924) suffered through the early travails of the modern ambiguity. In his stories, anxious individuals are at the mercy of an impersonal world. Walter Kaufman found a reference in one of Kafka's notebooks that suggests that in *The Castle*, God is dead, and humanity is left with a universe devoid of meaning and purpose. The novel begins by identifying Count Westwest as the occupant of the castle, but the Count is never mentioned again. What happened to the Count? Kafka's notebook says, 'The old count, to be sure, was dead, and so the young one should have reigned; but it was not that way: there was a *pause in history*, and the deputation went into *emptiness*'.[11]

Has something extraordinary happened to God? Has God changed—or has humanity merely changed its perception of God? Humanity's perception of the world has undergone profound changes over the centuries; therefore, it would seem reasonable to conclude that our *perception* of God should also have changed with the passage of time. Perhaps our perception of God is supposed to grow just as a child's relationship with its parents undergoes qualitative changes as the child develops from childhood to adolescence and then to maturity.[12]

Western history over the last millennium confirms the transition from the premodern era to the modern/postmodern era. The question is, "What is going to happen next?"

Late modern/postmodern thinkers have discredited modernity's early optimism just as modernity discredited the premodern hierarchies, and now everything is 'up in the air.' Some scholars view the new uncertainty as a permanent understanding, but perhaps it is just a temporary arrangement.[13]

Kafka's sketch describes the late modern/postmodern era as a "pause in history" where "emptiness" seems to have descended over Western civilization. The situation is reminiscent of the so-called "Iron Curtain" that descended across Europe and separated East and West during the Cold War. What happened to the certainty promised by premodern "authority" and modern "progress"? That certainty has been swept away by postmodern skepticism, and we are left with philosophical and theological

---

11. Kaufman, *Existentialism from Dostoyevsky to Sartre*, 122.
12. Geiger, *The Gospel According to Relativity*, 102–103.
13. Ibid., 193.

uncertainty regarding the meaning of life, itself, as well as our relationship with God.

However, acknowledging this "pause in history" may be the first step in reaffirming that God has revealed himself to his creation. Modernism discredited premodern blunders like the divine right of kings, white supremacy, and male chauvinism. Then postmodernism discredited modernism's arrogant assumptions regarding the inevitability of human progress. The demise of the old consensus ended the premodern certainty, and now we have a postmodern uncertainty that denies the possibility of a new consensus. Indeed, postmodern uncertainty has not only discredited the modern era but also produced a pause in history that looks a lot like chaos and decline.

The poet William Butler Yeats (1865–1939) used the metaphor of the falcon and the falconer to foreshadow an uncertain future, and his description seems to come into sharper focus with each succeeding decade. He said:

> Turning and turning in the widening gyre
> The falcon cannot hear the falconer;
> Things fall apart; the centre cannot hold.
> Mere anarchy is loosed upon the world,
> The blood-dimmed tide is loosed, and everywhere
> The ceremony of innocence is drowned;
> The best lack all conviction, while the worst
> Are full of passionate intensity.[14]

Society must develop a new consensus if it is going to avoid the "anarchy" that Yeats says has been "loosed upon the world." One need only follow the national and international news to see that the unmet political demands of the public can lead to violence and even anarchy.

As I said in opening this chapter, many people are tired of the uncertainty that is inherent in the late modern/postmodern agenda. But they are faced with a dilemma: They realize society cannot go back to the simplistic first wave that is associated with the premodern/early modern era. However, they also realize that we cannot continue with the second wave, that is, the growing chaos and uncertainty that are associated with the late modern/postmodern era. Therefore, they are waiting for a new rationale,

---

14. Yeats, "The Second Coming," 564.

Revelation: A New Perspective

that is, a third wave that will not only reaffirm divine revelation but also reestablish order and civility. (See Appendix Sec. 10.00)

This book challenges late modern/postmodern secularism by discussing revelation in the context of the theory of relativity. It may be true that relativity is a scientific theory, but it is also true that special and general relativity provide a unique model for discussing special and general revelation. Even more important, the relativity model recognizes that the constant Christ is the common denominator between special and general revelation just as the constant speed of light is the common denominator between special and general relativity.

I hasten to add that I am not the first evangelical Christian to suggest that relativity theory has something to contribute to the Christian tradition. Francis Schaeffer (1912–1984) was a strong proponent of historical Christianity, but he also recognized that a major transition was taking place in Western civilization. He was one of the first Christian leaders to acknowledge the modern challenge and to reexamine its impact on the contemporary church. In his first book *The God Who Is There*, he gave considerable thought to the relationship between human nature (what he called "the mannishness of man") and the nature of the universe.

Schaeffer studied modernity's problems as well as the possible solutions. He then boiled the possibilities down to four options, immediately dismissing the first three: He dismissed the idea that human beings are impersonal robots, that an impersonal universe could have produced personal human beings, and that the ultimate riddle of life lies somewhere out in the future. Schaeffer recognized, however, "That the scientific theory of relativity may in the future prove to be a sufficient answer for human life."[15] Of course, like secularists and many other Christians, Schaeffer stumbled over the confusing definitions that still cause people to think relativity and relativism mean the same thing. Most important, however, he understood the philosophical implication of the constant speed of light. [16]

My discussion of revelation and relativity is primarily directed toward the Judeo-Christian tradition, especially the Christian church as it struggles to understand its pluralistic position in a postmodern world. Indeed, one has to go all the way back to the first two centuries of the

---

15. Schaeffer, *The God Who Is There*, 111.
16. Geiger, *The Gospel According to Relativity*, 74–75.

early Church to find Christianity somewhat marginalized by religious pluralism.

Traditional Jews and many of my fellow Christians will reject or ignore the connection between revelation and relativity. Jews will dismiss relativity as irrelevant to Judaism, and Christians will criticize me for having "watered-down" the gospel. I pray, however, that both Jews and Christians will eventually realize that special relativity is consistent with each of their special traditions, and that the relativity perspective should be understood as a reaffirmation for each of their traditions.

Of course, many contemporary people have simply dismissed the idea of divine revelation. I hope, however, that my discussion of special and general revelation as modeled in special and general relativity will help skeptics realize that God is, that he has revealed himself in the person of Jesus Christ, and that the constant Christ is as real as the constant speed of light in $E=mc^2$.

9

The Relativity Model and Constant Value

Both the Christian worldview and the secular worldview have linked relativity and relativism together, as if they mean the same thing. Ironically, relativity and relativism are opposites—Relativity requires constant value, while relativism has no constant value.

MISUNDERSTANDING RELATIVITY

In recent years, both Christians and secularists have misinterpreted Albert Einstein's theory of relativity. That is, both sides subscribe to the erroneous idea that *relativity* and *relativism* are different ways of explaining the same concept.

On one hand, traditional Christians tend to resist the idea of relativity because they mistakenly associate relativity with relativism, and they know the floating values of modern relativism are incompatible with the eternal values of the Bible. Traditionalists know philosophical absolutism opposes philosophical relativism; therefore; they use absolutism with its "absolutes" to defend the Bible's eternal values. They *reject* the philosophical implications of "relativity" because they think relativism is the natural result of relativity.

On the other hand, late modern/postmodern secularists have rejected the Christian worldview in favor of a so-called scientific worldview.

And they think relativism is implicit in Einstein's relativity model. Secularists have capitulated to moral and ethical relativism because they believe relativity and relativism go together like the proverbial horse and carriage. They *accept* the philosophical implications of "relativity" because they think relativism is the natural result of relativity.

The situation has produced a strange commonality between the sacred and secular. The opposing sides misinterpret relativity in the same way. However, their opposing worldviews lead them to have opposite responses to relativity—One for and one against. Ironically, both sides make the same mistake but for different reasons.

In opposition to both of the above positions, I contend that relativity should be understood as a reaffirmation of eternal value. The new approach requires a rationale that is based upon the idea of "constant value" instead of the old absolutes—but the idea of eternal truth remains the same. Indeed, the biblical idea of eternal value is more consistent with the twenty-first-century idea of "constant value" than with the old absolutes that were used to justify the divine right of kings and white supremacy. As it turns out, the old absolutes were not so absolute after all. The obvious question is what are our values "relative to"?

Are all values simply relative to each other? Do particular values float from time to time and place to place with no overall frame of reference? Or, is there a philosophical frame of reference where particular values are relative to constant or eternal value? I call this scenario the "CTW Factor," that is, "Compared To What?" or "In Relationship to What?" For example, how does one compare the "goodness" of Mother Teresa and the "goodness" of fame and fortune? Compared to what?

Postmodernists Derrida and Eagleton, who were quoted earlier, have both used the term "relatively" in a friendly context. Derrida spoke of the "*relatively* unitary and atomic structures that are called names,"[1] and Eagleton said it is still possible for words to contain "*relatively* coherent meaning."[2] Like most late modern/postmodern writers, they have used the word "relatively" as an equivocation, as if it were a floating concept in which *all* values are "relative to each other."

---

1. Derrida, "Difference," 26.
2. Eagleton, *Literary Theory*, 111.

However, the late modern/postmodern perception of floating values is in direct conflict with the ideas of Galileo (1564–1642), Isaac Newton (1642–1727), and Albert Einstein (1879–1955):

Galileo originated the principle of "relativity," that is, the idea that being "relative to" meant that a person's point of view was relative to a fixed frame of reference. For example, looking out of my train toward the train on the next track in a huge railway terminal, it was impossible for me to determine which train was beginning to move out of the station—until I saw the ground. I was the observer, and my connection with the ground gave me a "fixed" point from which to determine that the other train was moving away from me.

With Newton's classical physics, the scientist is the observer who always occupies a "fixed" point of observation. In other words, Newton's scientific calculations assume that the observer is standing still, as if he has stepped away from the earth's rotation onto a platform or a "skyhook" that is fixed in space. With its fixed frame of reference, Newtonian physics dominated science for over two hundred years until the Einsteinian revolution eliminated the idea of a fixed frame of reference.

Science now realizes that everything in the universe is in motion and that the earlier idea of a fixed point in space was an illusion. With Einstein's new physics, both the scientific observer *and* the object being observed are in motion, along with all the other parts of the universe. The genius of Einstein is that his scientific calculations assume that the scientific observer must forgo Newton's "skyhook" and stay on the rotating, orbiting earth. Needless to say, the fact that both the observer and the object being observed are in motion complicates the mathematical calculations. But it provides a more realistic scenario of the moving parts of the world in which we live. A detailed analysis of Einstein's theory of relativity is beyond the scope of this study, but I have tried to conceptualize the basic components of the theory of relativity in the Appendix. (See Appendix, Sec. 3:00, Sec. 4:00, Sec. 5.00, and Sec. 6:00)

Premodern cosmology thought God had "fixed" the earth in place at the center of the universe, and that the sun, moon, and stars were circling the earth. Galileo used a primitive telescope to confirm Copernicus's (1473–1543) theory that the earth was not the center of the universe, thereby disproving the "old" cosmology. However, the "new" cosmology adopted a model that said God had "fixed" the sun, rather than the earth, at the center of the universe and that the earth, moon, and stars were "relative to" the sun.

Contemporary cosmology now tells us there is no fixed point in the universe, that everything in the universe is in motion, and that the universe is actually expanding. However, does this cosmological state of motion support the late modern/postmodern idea that moral and ethical values are constantly changing? In other words, are the moral and ethical values of each individual "relative to" the moral and ethical values of other people or are they "relative to" eternal values?

THE NATURE OF RELATIVITY

When properly understood, the theory of relativity not only modifies early scientific ideas but also discredits the relativism that is inherent in the late modern/postmodern point of view. Looking back over the history of ideas, it is easy to see that science has always had considerable impact on philosophy and theology.

The *premodern mistake* in philosophy and theology was to follow early scientists (or natural philosophers as they were called) in assuming the existence of a fixed frame of reference. Those early scholars thought human experience had to be "relative to" a fixed frame of reference just as the universe was thought to be "relative to" the fixed earth and later the fixed sun. Predictably, the early philosophers and theologians followed the early scientists and assumed the existence of fixed or absolute ideas. Beginning with Greek philosophy, especially the ideas of Aristotle, philosophers relied upon a hierarchy of absolutes to establish a fixed frame of reference. Acknowledging God as the Supreme Being, early theologians followed early scientists and mistakenly theorized that God's preeminence "fixed" him at the top of a spiritual hierarchy. However, as part of the theory of relativity, Einstein determined that the universe is a moving frame of reference; that is, everything is in either uniform motion or nonuniform motion. Therefore, the idea of a fixed frame of reference is false.

The *modern/postmodern mistake* in philosophy and theology has been to misconstrue Einstein's moving frame of reference. Because science has determined that the physical world is changing, secular humanists have jumped to the mistaken conclusion that moral and ethical values change as well. However, in addition to the moving frame, Einstein

The Relativity Model and Constant Value

determined that both uniform motion and non-uniform motion are "relative to" the constant speed of light. Instead of having *no* frame of reference, we have a *moving* frame of reference where variable motions are "relative to" the speed of light. The idea that moral and ethical values change from time to time and place to place is not only false but also disastrous because it has led to modern/postmodern relativism.

Whereas traditional theists cling to the erroneous notion of a fixed frame of reference, most non-theists have jumped to the equally erroneous conclusion that we have *no* frame of reference. It is incorrect, therefore, to treat the old idea of a fixed frame of reference and the new idea of having no frame of reference as opposite sides of the same coin. Instead, each one is scientifically false.

The truth is that both the premodern philosophy of *absolutism* (fixed frame) and the modern/postmodern philosophy of *relativism* (no frame) have missed the mark. On one hand, absolutism was mistaken about the existence of a fixed frame of reference. On the other hand, relativism compounded the earlier mistake by jumping to the conclusion that having *no fixed* frame of reference meant having *no* frame of reference whatsoever.

When correctly understood, Einstein's theory of relativity undermines moral and ethical relativism. A superficial understanding of relativity might seem to justify relativism by suggesting that every motion is relative to every other motion. However, a deeper understanding of the relativity model with its moving frame of reference shows that both uniform motion and non-uniform motion are ultimately relative to constant value as with the constant speed of light in $E=mc^2$. (See Appendix Sec. 6.00)

Ironically, Eagleton tried to use the idea of a flickering light, as previously quoted, to describe the illusive nature of language and meaning.[3] But his "constant flickering" is a perfect picture of a strobe light that uses the speed of light to illuminate that which cannot be seen with the naked eye, like moving dancers in a dark room or a timing mark on a spinning flywheel.

The scientific explanation is that everything *is* in motion, but the constancy of the speed of light mediates between uniform motion and non-uniform motion. Properly stated, "uniform motion and non-uniform motion" are not relative to each other, but are part of a "moving frame of

---

3. Ibid., 128.

reference" in which *all* forms of motion are relative to the "constant speed of light."

Indeed, the constant speed of light is the common denominator that allows astronomers to study the sun and the planets within our galaxy, as well as the stars located many light years away. Understanding the speed of light makes space travel possible and accounts for the precise calculations that enable a space capsule to enter earth's tiny space window instead of bouncing off in space or flaming out on reentry to earth's atmosphere.

I would argue, therefore, that the late modern/postmodern practice of interpreting "relative to" as relativism is a serious misnomer and should be avoided. Instead, "relative to" should be understood in the context of relativity where the constant speed of light is a symbol for constant value.

RELATIVITY AND CONSTANT VALUE

If moral and ethical values were subject to change from time to time and place to place, there would be no room for the eternal values that are inherent in Christianity. However, if the relativity model confirms the existence of constant value then it is a reaffirmation of the eternal or universal values at the heart of the gospel of Jesus Christ. The real issue, however, is not the existence of a theistic worldview, but whether a person's response to God has any impact on the way he or she lives at home and in the marketplace. Religiosity rings hollow when a person's behavior is inconsistent with social justice and loving relationships.

If one thinks in terms of the relativity model, instead of the subjective ponderings of today's intelligentsia, then "relative to" should be understood to mean that human beings are *relative to constant value* rather than relative to each other—just as uniform motion and non-uniform motion are *relative to the constant speed of light* as in $E=mc^2$.

Whereas Derrida and other postmodernists dispute the existence of universal value, the relativity model is consistent with the traditional idea of universal value:

In philosophical terms, the uniformity of "self" and the non-uniformity of "other" are *relative to* the abstract idea of constant value ("c"). I cannot give a comprehensive definition of justice, but I recognize injustice when I see it. Humanly speaking, my personal uniformity (self) and the non-uniformity of my wife (other) are relative to each other, but in relationship to eternity, each of us is *relative to* eternal value ("c") that is beyond our finite understanding. Indeed, who can fathom the love that binds one to a spouse or a child? With the relativity model, self and other are ultimately "relative to" constant or eternal value, and that is radically different from relativism's erroneous idea that self and other are only "relative to" each other.

In theological terms, my uniformity (self) and the non-uniformity of my wife (other) are *relative to the constant Christ* ("c") who is "the same yesterday and today, yes and forever" (Heb 13:8). Who can comprehend the gulf that separates the holiness of divine perfection from humanity's imperfection? Only a divine mediator could bridge the gap between God and humanity. The Bible says God-as-Son intervened in human history in the person of Jesus Christ in order to serve as the ultimate mediator between human uniformity and divine non-uniformity (John 3:16).

Of course, the sword cuts both ways. The relativity model rejects the modern/postmodernism aversion to universal value, but it also rejects traditional Christianity's oversimplification of universal value. Without question, the Christian tradition has a fondness for the old absolutes. Unfortunately, that old fixed frame mentality perpetuates the either/or dualism that forces "absolute" value onto one side of each duality. The curse of the old dualism is that it led to philosophical and theological blunders like white supremacy and the divine right of kings.

Perhaps it is only the "fixed frame of reference" of the old absolutism that has been discredited by Derrida, Eagleton, and others—a feat that Einstein demonstrated when he established that there is no such thing as absolute rest in the temporal world. If everything in the world were in motion, then the idea of "rest" would have to be outside the worldly realm of time and space. As the writer of Hebrews said, "Therefore, let us fear lest, while a promise remains of entering *His rest*, any one of you should seem to have come short of it" (Heb 4:1).

FROM TRADITIONAL ABSOLUTISM TO CONSTANT VALUE

Admittedly, the modern/postmodern critique has damaged philosophical absolutism. First, the critique undermined political "absolutes" like the divine right of kings, then it undermined social "absolutes" like white supremacy, and now it has called into question theological "absolutes" like the existence of God and the authority of the Bible.

It should be noted, however, that absolutism with its fixed frame of reference is merely a school of philosophy. The passage of time and the development of fresh ideas may have discredited the rationale of absolutism, but the existence of God and the inherent truth of the Bible have not been discredited.

Unfortunately, the dismantling of the old absolutes has left moral and ethical relativism as the default position where meaning has no frame of reference. In a rather short period of time, the new relativism has destabilized meaning and created philosophical and theological uncertainty regarding the meaning of right and wrong and good and evil.

Now the meaning of eternal truth must be re-stabilized relative to the constant Christ who is "the same yesterday and today, yes and forever." The relativity model not only agrees that the discredited old "absolutes" are not eternal, but also reconfirms the existence of eternal value as represented in the constant value of $E=mc^2$. Indeed, the relativity model and constant value are perfectly at home with the moving frame of reference that is also associated with the modern/postmodern world.

Furthermore, the free space velocity of light (c) is not the only constant that science has identified. Max Planck (1858–1947) began the transition from classical physics to quantum theory in 1900 with "Planck's constant" (h). Planck's pioneer work in quantum physics was instrumental in the discovery of a scientific formula that uses h as a mathematical constant to explain that radiation is "emitted and received" from atoms in separate bundles or packets called "quanta."[4] Five years later, following Planck's lead, Einstein used the constant speed of light (c) to develop the special theory of relativity with its formula of $E=mc^2$.

Einstein used Planck's quantum theory to describe the physical characteristics of light and to show that the free space velocity of light ("c") is constant even in a moving frame of reference. Next to the constant speed of light in $E=mc^2$, "Planck's constant" is probably the most notable constant in modern science. The speed of light (c) and these quantum packets (h) are recognized constants in the scientific world, and they are accompanied by the law of gravity and certain other forces of nature that confirm the existence of constant value.

4. Ludwig, "Max Planck," 261.

The Relativity Model and Constant Value

The physical reality that constant value in the scientific world reaches out beyond human understanding seems to substantiate the existence of a spiritual reality that reaches out beyond human understanding. The situation is as if God has out-sourced constant value to a scientific dimension in order to corroborate the constant Christ as part of a spiritual reality that is beyond human understanding.

I am reminded of my own school days when a seventh grade classmate asked the science teacher—"Who passed the law of gravity?" Everybody laughed, including the teacher. Mrs. Jamison didn't have an answer then, and the scientific establishment doesn't have an answer today! The fact is that scientists do not understand *how* or *why* these scientific values or "laws" are constant. God seems to have provided circumstantial evidence regarding his existence, and the case has now gone to the jury, so to speak. Each "juror" must make a decision regarding the truth that has been made known to him. Indeed, one's response to God is not only an individual matter but also part of a collective decision that impacts other people.

Postmodernism may have devalued the traditional confidence in language, as such, but language is only the tip of the iceberg. The issue is not whether language is a limited process in which meaning has a precarious attachment to truth. The fact is that our understanding of the whole universe is a limited process. Like every other aspect of human existence, language is part of a mysterious moving frame of reference. The limited nature of human experience is a given, and everyone must play the hand he or she is dealt in terms of gene pool, environment, and culture.

However, postmodernism's devaluation and, at times, denigration of language begs the question. The issue is not *whether* human language is limited, but *how* one is going to respond to his or her limitations. Admittedly, neither written nor spoken language can fully express conscious intent ("How much do you love your children?") or explain the internal baggage that people carry around ("I wonder what she meant by that!"). But late modern/postmodern relativism is not the solution to society's problems. Language is a God-given tool that helps us plumb the depths of our relationships with each other and with God. We don't know everything, but we know enough to respond to God's revelation.

In summarizing the relativity mode, I can report that at least one distinguished scholar has agreed with my distinction between relativity and relativism. In 2006, a mutual friend recommended my book *The*

Gospel According to Relativity to Dr. L. Russ Bush (1944–2008), Southeastern Baptist Theological Seminary professor of Christian Philosophy and the first Director of Southeastern's Center for Faith and Culture. Dr. Bush read and then reviewed my book on his website. (See Appendix Sec. 11.00)

He was also kind enough to send me his book *The Advancement: Keeping the Faith in an Evolutionary Age*, and we discussed the relationship between relativity and relativism. After exchanging a few emails, he agreed with the following restatement regarding the relativity mode:

> The pure subjectivity of truth requires the willingness to trust the subjectivity of other people's perceptions, perceptions that are solely relative to each other—as in the moral and cultural relativism of ideas and values. A deeper understanding of reality leads to the acknowledgement of the relativity mode where individual perceptions are relative to the constant value of Christ as exemplified in the constant speed of light. While the objectivity of the natural world is widely accepted as being self-evident, such a claim cannot be known to be the case if there is no reference point outside of the individual consciousness at which or by which to compare the thoughts of reality.[5]

Dr. Bush was a well known scholar. Therefore, his support for the work of an unknown layman probably says more about his exemplary character than it says about the layman. Nevertheless, his approval has been a continuing source of encouragement to me.

---

5. Bush, *The Advancement*, 122.

10

Constant Value and the Constant Christ

Each person is accountable to God for the divine revelation he or she has received just as each one has to navigate the circumstances of his or her life. However, should our understanding of God's ultimate revelation be limited to a first century metaphor where Christ is identified with the "cornerstone" of a building? Or should we expand our understanding of revelation by using a twenty-first-century metaphor where the "constant Christ" is identified with the constant speed of light as in $E=mc^2$. After all, Jesus said, "I am the light of the world."

WHAT DO WE KNOW?

What God knows about us is infinitely more important than what we know about God. I am reminded of a story about a wealthy oilman who was buying a high-priced sports car. When he asked about the horsepower of the engine, the salesman explained that the company didn't give out horsepower specifications. The affluent buyer was used to having his way in such matters, so he said he would not buy the car unless he received the factory's assurance that the engine had adequate horsepower. Trying to protect his commission, the anxious salesman sent an email to the home office explaining the situation and asking "how much" horsepower the engine had. When the salesman and his customer read the reply, it simply said, *"Enough"!* Spiritually speaking, how much do we need to know about God? We need to know *enough* to respond to his initiatives.

God has revealed himself "in many portions and in many ways," and especially "in His Son" (Heb 1:1–2). The real issue, however, is not the extent of our knowledge, but whether God exists, whether he has intervened in human history, and whether we have responded to the revelation we have received. More specifically, has God revealed himself in and through Jesus Christ, and have we responded to that revelation?

THE HUMANISTIC ERROR

One will have completely missed the point if he or she tries to idealize "constant value" by identifying it with the human endeavors that are associated with altruism and good works in general. Humanity represents the limited side of the classification model that differentiates between humanity's finite imperfection and God's infinite perfection.

The humanistic temptation is to identify constant value with human reason. But to identify "constant value" in humanistic terms is to assume the autonomy of the individual, that is, to suggest a "self-help" mentality where the individual tries to overcome his own imperfection. To equate constant value with temporal values makes humanity (individually or collectively) the ultimate measure of value and perpetuates the human pride that C.S. Lewis called an "anti-God state of mind."[1]

Furthermore, it doesn't help to use the pretty face of "freedom" to paint over the ugly face of sin. With God, there is no difference between the "old" autonomy of sinful disobedience and the "modern" autonomy of human freedom.

The so-called freedom of the late modern/postmodern mind is seen in the Nietzschean mindset where God is passé and the individual conscience is the ultimate "measure of value." Claiming "superiority" and an "independent" will, Nietzsche's "sovereign man" supposedly exercises his "unbreakable will" and achieves "mastery over circumstances, over nature, and over all more short-willed and unreliable creatures."[2]

---

1. Lewis, *Mere Christianity*, 122.
2. Nietzsche, *Basic Writing of Nietzsche*, 494–496.

Instead of relying solely on human reason, constant value is more properly identified with justice and love. As the prophet Micah said, "And what does the Lord require of you But to do justice, to love kindness, And to walk humbly with your God?" (Mic 6:8)? The reality is that the secular humanist must either force science to overreach its finite bounds or engage in pure speculation in order to "explain" the mysteries of a universe that extends beyond the finite horizon of human knowledge. After all, how does one account for the constant speed of light or Planck's constant? And who "passed" the law of gravity?

THE NATURE OF SPIRITUALITY

Constant value is independent from both sides of the uniformity and non-uniformity model. In science, the relativity model says the constant speed of light is independent of both uniform and non-uniform motion. In Christian theology, the suffering Christ was independent of heaven and earth. Indeed, Jesus was physically suspended between heaven and earth. He suffered earthly anguish when his fellow human beings betrayed him—And he suffered heavenly agony when he cried out, "My God, My God, why hast Thou forsaken Me" (Matt 27:46).

The Christian message is that the constant Christ looked "down" from the cross at the imperfect people who had rejected him and "up" to the divine perfection that had forsaken him, and he was alone! Even the shape of the cross demonstrates that Christ was suspended between heaven and earth as the ultimate "middleman." Jesus said, "as Moses lifted up the serpent in the wilderness, even so must the Son of Man be lifted up (John 3:14). In his passion, Christ was truly independent from both human uniformity and divine non-uniformity, just as the speed of light is independent from uniform motion and non-uniform motion.

Anyone who has ever been rejected or betrayed by a friend can identify, to some extent, with the way Christ was treated by his countrymen. Given the nature of political power and the content of the gospel message, it was a foregone conclusion that Jesus would eventually be isolated from his fellow human beings.

But why was Jesus isolated from God? Why did he cry out, "My God, my God, why hast thou forsaken me?" I would argue that the explanation is found in the holiness that separates divine *perfection* and human *imperfection*, a separation that grows out of human accountability. As discussed earlier, perfection and imperfection are like oil and water; they simply do not mix. Indeed, if perfection and imperfection were fused, then "perfection" would no longer be perfect.

The dilemma of juxtaposing perfection and imperfection is as if an infant's diaper were soiled so badly that the child could not be cleaned. Imagine for a moment that the qualitative nature of the filth is such that no known cleanser is capable of removing the stench. Now assume that a supernatural father is able to remove his right arm and transform it into an extraordinary fabric that absorbs the filth and purifies the child. The arm has the innate form of the father, but it takes on the outward fashion of a fabric in order to cleanse the child. The filth, of course, makes the "arm" unacceptable to the father. Indeed, the filth brings death to the "arm"—But death, itself, is defeated after being in the grave for three days. So after seventy-two hours, the father brings this extraordinary fabric out of the ground as pristine as ever. Having been restored to its original purity, the fabric is transformed back into a right arm and returned to its place of honor with the father.

From the beginning, God's perfection meant that something would have to be done about the sinful imperfection that he knew would result from human freedom. Indeed, the confrontation between perfection and imperfection presented an extraordinary set of circumstances:

> Divine Perfection
> Perfect knowledge prevented the unawareness *of* sin,
> Perfect justice required accountability *for* sin, but
> Perfect love provided a remedy *from* sin.

The perfect justice of God-as-Father could not tolerate sin—But the perfect love of God-as-Son stepped into the broken relationship between the prefect creator and the fallen and now imperfect creature. Like a sponge removing dirt from the floor, the "only begotten" assumed responsibility for the sin of the whole world. As the prophet Isaiah said seven hundred years before Christ, "All we like sheep have gone astray; we have turned every one to his own way; and the Lord hath laid on him the iniquity of us all" (Isa 53:6 KJV). Jesus Christ, as the only begotten, was the catalyst that solved the sin problem between God and humanity.

THE RELATIONSHIP BETWEEN SELF AND OTHER

The uniformity/non-uniformity model mirrors the relationship between human uniformity (self) and the non-uniformity of God (Eternal Other), but it also addresses the self/other relationships that exist between and among human beings. In these human relationships, each person is both uniformity and non-uniformity. That is, each individual has a double perspective—each one is both self and other.

For example, from the first perspective, I am *uniformity*—the self-interest side of the model. The uniformity of my self-interest includes my individual subjectivity, as well as the collective subjectivity of the groups to which I belong. I belong to small groups like my family, my law firm, and my church as well as large groups such as race, country, culture, and religion. Belonging to multiple groups creates overlapping layers of self-interest and bias. Indeed, the layered effect complicates human experience and even institutionalizes problems like racism, sexism, and class-consciousness. Of course, the ultimate uniformity is being a human being compared to the ultimate reality of God's non-uniformity.

From the second perspective, I am *non-uniformity*—that is, the non-uniform "other" to the uniformity of someone else's self-interest. The uniformity/non-uniformity model remains the same, but the parties change sides. Suddenly, I find myself on the other side of the same equation—The insider has become an outsider! All human beings are caught up in the limitations of time, place, and circumstances, and all of our perceptions, whether as "self" or "other," are filtered through a multitude of human variables. As a practical matter, I should never be intolerant of another person because I am non-uniform to his or her uniformity.

All human preferences and decisions are somewhat suspect because: (1) the "self" of each perspective always has a vested interest in itself, (2) the "other" of each perspective is just a self-interested "self" from the opposite perspective, and (3) all of our thoughts and feelings are constantly changing and evolving. With all the mixed motives and changing attitudes, it is no wonder good relationships are difficult to establish and sustain.

The good news for the twenty-first century is that the "c" in the theory of relativity can be understood as a symbol for value that does not change. The constant value of "c" transcends the human variables of self and other (uniformity and non-uniformity) and brings bias and self-interest out in the open.

Whether one realizes it or not, the relativity model means that every decision he or she makes is related to a complex system of temporal relationships that are in a state of flux. Each decision is made in the context of individual self-interests and the collective self-interests of each group to which he or she belongs. Each decision is also made in the context of the personal and collective interests of other individuals and their groups. In other words, the model forces one to contemplate all of the various aspects of the self/other equation. The Bible says Cain asked the famous question, "Am I my brother's keeper?" Maybe it would be more precise to say, "Am I my other's keeper?"

Ultimately, the relativity model means all of our decisions are *relative to* "c"—that is, constant value that does not change. Indeed, when one contemplates the reality of eternity, he or she becomes more aware of the transient nature of temporal relationships and values. In Christian terms, an imperfect creature (finite self) is accountable to the perfect Creator (infinite Other), but that accountability is mediated through the constant Christ ("c"). So what do we know about Christ, and why should we refer to him as the constant Christ?

FROM CORNERSTONE TO THE CONSTANT CHRIST

Most people, including scholarly experts, realize that something extraordinary is happening within Western civilization. Indeed, Christianity is faced with a socio-political transition that includes a shift from traditional Christian values to the secular values of a "post-Christian" society. The Christian challenge is to communicate the story of Jesus and his love to an audience that is increasingly secular and scientific.

This book is an attempt to meet that challenge by doing two things simultaneously: First, it reaffirms the first century reality of the eternal Christ. Second, it presents the eternal Christ in a way that can be understood by a twenty-first-century audience. However, to accomplish the task, the book must make a connection between the Bible's first century explanation of constant value and the contemporary understanding of constant value.

One way to make that connection is to build a bridge between the first century worldview and the twenty-first-century worldview. For example, is there any linkage between the biblical description of Christ as a "cornerstone" and a twenty-first-century association of Christ with the "constant speed of light"? And if so, what difference does it make?

From the first century to the twentieth century, time and space were understood as absolute. Time was an ever flowing river that moved from past, to present, to future, and the world was understood as having a fixed frame of reference. As previously discussed, the earth and later the sun were understood to be fixed at the center of the universe. Constancy meant that buildings were constructed on solid ground rather than on shifting sand. The foundation of each building was fixed in place beginning with the "cornerstone," and the rest of the work had to be carried out relative to that first stone. The same principle applies when laying kitchen tile; the first tile sets the arrangement for everything that follows.

It was perfectly natural, therefore, for biblical writers to use the cornerstone as a metaphor for the constancy of eternal value and eventually for the constancy of Christ himself. The practice began in the Old Testament. In the Book of Job, God was referring to the foundation of the earth when he said, "On what were its bases sunk? Or who laid its cornerstone?" Later, the Psalmist said, "The stone which the builders rejected has become the chief corner stone." And Isaiah said, "Behold I am laying in Zion a stone, a tested stone, a costly cornerstone for the foundation, firmly placed" (Job 38:6, Ps 118:22, Isa 28:16).

The New Testament continued the cornerstone metaphor as pertaining to Jesus and his eternal status. In Mark's gospel, Jesus referred to himself as the cornerstone when he said, "The stone which the builders rejected, This became the chief corner stone." The theme is repeated in both Matthew and Luke. In Acts, Peter was referring to Jesus when he said, "He is the stone which was rejected by you, the builders, but which became the very corner stone. And there is salvation in no one else; for there is no other name under heaven that has been given among men by which we must be saved." Following Isaiah, the apostle Paul said, "So then, you are no longer strangers and aliens, but you are fellow-citizens with the saints, and are of God's household, having been built upon the foundation of the apostles and prophets, Christ Jesus Himself being the corner stone, in whom the whole building, being fitted together is growing into a holy temple in the Lord; in whom you also are being built together into a dwelling of God in the Spirit." And Peter followed both Isaiah and the Psalmist when he said, "Behold I lay in Zion a choice stone, a precious corner stone, and he who believes in Him shall not be disappointed. This precious value, then, is for you who believe, but for those who disbelieve, the stone which the builders rejected, This became the very corner stone, and a stone of stumbling and a rock of offense" (Mark 12:10, Matt 21:42, Luke 22:17, Acts 4:11–12, Eph 2:19–22, 1 Pet 22:6–8).

SPIRITUAL TRANSITION TO NEW ERA

Perhaps the most difficult of all historical transitions is the spiritual shift from one era to another. We see it in the transition from the Roman gods to apostolic Christianity, to the early Catholic era, to the Roman Catholic/Orthodox eras, to the Protestant era, and now to the modern/postmodern era. Each transition plays out over an extended period of time and has extraordinary and sometimes violent impact on both insiders and outsiders. One need only study the Protestant Reformation and the Thirty Years War to verify Europe's volatility during the sixteenth and seventeenth centuries. In recent years, historical Christianity has been relentlessly challenged by the development of science and technology as well as the "modern" idea that there is a discrepancy between science and Christianity.

However, if God created the natural world, there can be no discrepancy between his creation of that world and his self-revelation to that world. Jesus acknowledged that his disciples would have trouble in the world, but he said, "I have overcome the world" (John 16:33). Indeed, the gospel is built around the extraordinary claim that God raised Jesus from the dead as the ultimate victory over the temporal world. As the apostle Paul said, "Death is swallowed up in victory. O death, where is your victory? O death, where is your sting?" (1 Cor 15:54–55).

In view of Jesus' portrayal of himself as "the light of the world" and the claim in Heb 13:8 that he is the same yesterday, today, and forever, I would argue that the "constant speed of light" is now a more viable metaphor for Christ than a first century "cornerstone." Indeed, the constant speed of light confirms the constancy of the old cornerstones. Contemporary Christians should understand the constant Christ in relationship to the nature of light, itself, as well as the traditional idea of spiritual illumination.

FROM RELATIVITY TO REVELATION

Perhaps the most radical aspect of the relativity model is the suggestion that the constant Christ is the common denominator between both special revelation *and* general revelation—just as the constant speed of light ("c") is the common denominator between special relativity *and* general relativity. But, what does it mean to say that the constant Christ is a common referent for both special and general revelation?

The scientific fact that the constant speed of light ("c") is the natural connection between special relativity and general relativity is the basis for the theological analogy that says the constant Christ ("c") is the spiritual connection between special revelation and general revelation. When Christ is understood as the connection between special revelation *and* general revelation, then traditional Christology will have been expanded exponentially.

However, the extended Christology requires that we reexamine the limitations that some have imposed on Christ's atonement. In other words, why is Christ's atonement limited to those who are privy to the new covenant? On what biblical basis, one might ask, can it be argued that Christ's atonement might be available not only to the insiders who are privy to the new covenant but also to some non-covenant outsiders who were or are strangers to the new covenant? My first impulse was to look to those in the past who have struggled with the mystery of God's providence.

For example, after dealing at length with personal pain and suffering, Job said, "I have declared that which I did not understand, Things too wonderful for me, which I did not know . . . I have heard of Thee by the hearing of the ear; But now my eye sees Thee; Therefore I *retract*, and I *repent* in dust and ashes" (Job 42:3, 5).

From chapter 9 through chapter 11 of Romans, the apostle Paul struggled mightily with the enigma of God's irrevocable commitment to Israel and Israel's rejection of Jesus as Messiah. Having poured out his soul, the apostle fell back on divine providence and said, "How unsearchable are His judgments and unfathomable His ways. For who has known the mind of the Lord, or who became His counselor ... For from Him and through Him and to Him are all things" (11:33-36).

In chapters 12 and 13 of 1 Corinthians, Paul went to great lengths to explain the spiritual gifts and to pen the magnificent "love chapter." But he acknowledged his own limitations when he said, "For we know in part, and we prophesy in part; but when the perfect comes, the partial will be done away. When I was a child, I used to speak as a child, think as a child, reason as a child; when I became a man, I did away with childish things. For now we see in a mirror dimly, but then face to face; now I know in part, but then I shall know fully just as I also have been fully known" (1 Cor 13:9-12).

The writer of Acts reminded us that King David died "after he had served the purpose of God *in his own generation*" (Acts 13:36). I would argue, therefore, that other generations can also have unique responsibilities. As contemporary Christians, we must search the depth and breadth of God's Word in order to serve his purpose in our generation. The ultimate issue is whether God's grace as seen in Christ's atonement is limited to people who are privy to the biblical covenants or is that grace unbounded.

The apostle Paul had to deal with a malicious misrepresentation of his ministry where some critics tried to associate him with the idea that a believer could "continue in sin" because that would increase God's grace. Dismissing their foolishness, he said, "Are we to continue in sin that grace might increase? May it never be! How shall we who died to sin still live in it" (Rom 6:1-2)?

But the apostle did not back away from the previous two verses regarding the unlimited nature of divine grace. Indeed, he was unequivocal in Rom 5:20-21 when he said, "And the Law came in that the transgression might increase, but where sin increased, grace abounded all the more, that, as sin reigned in death, even so grace might reign through righteousness to eternal life through Jesus Christ our Lord." Paul said the extent of the sin problem is only exceeded by the magnitude of the grace of God that is manifested through Jesus Christ.

We know from Rom 3:20 that the law brings "knowledge of sin" for *all* people and from Rom 3:23 that "*all* have sinned." Therefore, we must conclude that since, under the law, sin increases to include *all* people, so grace increases "all the more" for *all* people. So who has access to God's grace, and are there any third party beneficiaries?

11

Faith of Jesus Christ

Generations of theologians have struggled to understand the full nature of God's grace. Catholic theology says salvation is bound up in the sacraments of the church. In Protestantism, the Reform tradition says salvation is a matter of divine election where regeneration precedes repentance, and the Arminian tradition says salvation is related to personal repentance and having faith in Jesus Christ. What is the ultimate source of salvation, and what is the connection between the Son's atonement and the Father's forgiveness?

INTRODUCTION

The Apostle Paul confirmed the source of salvation when he said the "righteousness of God" is manifested through the "faith *of* Jesus Christ" (Rom 3:21–22 KJV). Some scholars believe the King James Version is more accurate than later translations on this point, because it attaches salvation to the faith "*of* Jesus Christ." In other words, saving faith is based solely on who Christ is and what he has done.

In stark contrast to the King James translation, most of the modern translations say the "righteousness of God" is manifested through one's "faith *in* Jesus Christ." However, having "faith *in* Jesus Christ" creates the impression that salvation is based upon what a human being does, that is, by placing his or her faith or trust *in* Christ.

Understanding the difference between the "faith *of* Christ" and having "faith *in* Christ" is essential. The faith of Christ is a divine activity, whereas, having faith in Christ is a human activity. So what is the difference?

Faith is active in the sense that it is something one does. For example, faith signals a confidence in having the *ability* to accomplish something on one's own. Faith can cause a person to board an airplane. But it is a radically different power that lifts that airplane into the air. Faith can cause a person to respond to the gospel story, to attend church, and to pray. But the grace of God is the only power capable of lifting the burden of sin. As Jesus said, he came "to seek and to save that which was lost" (Luke 19:10). Having faith in Christ is important in connection with the lifelong journey of sanctification, that is, where a person is privy to the gospel and has the opportunity to grow in the nurture and admonition of the Lord.

Repentance, however, is passive in the sense that I don't have the power to contribute in any way to my salvation. Indeed, repentance signals my *inability* to save myself and indicates that I have humbled myself in the presence of almighty God. Philosophically and theologically, repentance means unconditional surrender. As discussed earlier, the situation is as if I were running down a dark alley, came up against a brick wall, and realized I have no way to escape. I cannot save myself or even contribute to my own rescue.

Furthermore, repentance is not salvific. It merely neutralizes the finite will. Surrendering one's will to the heavenly Father is sort of like a child surrendering her will to an earthly father. Indeed, Jesus even said, ". . . unless you are converted and become like children, you shall not enter the kingdom of heaven. Whoever then humbles himself as this child, he is the greatest in the kingdom of heaven" (Matt 18:3–4). How is faith related to God's forgiveness?

SUBJECTIVE GENITIVE VS. OBJECTIVE GENITIVE

Having studied Rom 3:22 and the rest of the Book of Romans for many years, I thought I was alone in seeing a theological distinction between the "faith *of* Jesus Christ" in the King James translation and the idea of putting one's "faith *in* Jesus Christ" as seen in most modern translations.

However, I recently found in David H. Stern's *Jewish New Testament Commentary* an extended discussion of the "faith of Jesus Christ."[1] Stern is a Messianic Jew and a Bible scholar who translates "*dia pisteos Iesou Christou*" as "through the faithfulness of Yeshua the Messiah."[2] Yeshua, of course, is the Hebrew word for Jesus. (See Appendix Sec. 7.00)

Since discovering Stern's commentary, I have learned that the distinction between the "faith of Christ" and having "faith in Christ" is the subject of a wide-ranging debate.

It seems that Rom 3:22 contains an ambiguity that is built into the Greek text. Furthermore, the same usage appears in at least eight other places in Paul's letters, and intellectual honesty requires that they be translated in the same manner. (See Rom 3:26, Gal 2:16 (twice), 3:22, Eph 3:12, and Phil 3:9, Col 2:12 and 2 Thess 2:13) If we subscribe to the idea that the Bible is divinely inspired, then we must conclude that the ambiguity is not a mistake and that it serves a useful purpose. However, the translator carries a heavy burden because he or she must make a grammatical decision by choosing between the "objective genitive" (faith in Christ) and the "subjective genitive" (faith of Christ). But what difference does it make?

In English, the difference between the subjective case and objective case can be understood from watching a baseball game—That is, did "John hit the ball," or did "the ball hit John"? The subjective case means John delivers the action by "hitting the ball." The objective case means John receives the action. He is the object that is "hit by the ball."

The issue is in choosing between the subjective genitive and the objective genitive when translating *dia pisteos Iesou Christou* in Rom 3:22. The subjective case is translated "by faith of Jesus Christ" while the objective case is translated "through faith in Jesus Christ."[3] The Greek text supports either translation; therefore, the ambiguity must be resolved by studying the overall passage. Paul's sentence structure forces a translator to analyze this text in light of the larger context, and then to choose between the subjective and the objective.

---

1. Stern, *Jewish New Testament Commentary*, 347–348, 538–540.
2. Stern, Translator, *Complete Jewish Bible*, 1405.
3. Ibid., 348.

Stern discusses the opposing translations in a way that is easily accessible to both scholars and general readers. He readily acknowledges that in most modern versions of the Bible, *"dia pisteos Iesou Christou"* is translated "through faith *in* Jesus Christ" (Rom 3:22). We have to conclude, therefore, that the use of the objective genitive is the majority rule. Stern contends, however, that the objective genitive is suspect because it says, "God considers an individual righteous *because* he [the individual] believes in Yeshua."[4]

The objective case means the "righteousness of God" is somehow manifested by or through the finite faith that a human being has in Jesus Christ. The crucial issue is whether a believer's salvation is based on the faithfulness of Christ, himself, or the faithfulness of various believers who have varying degrees of knowledge regarding the gospel message.

Cutting to the core issue, Stern says, "Subjective genitive means that the faith/faithfulness is Yeshua's own faith in and faithfulness to God his Father, not our faith in Yeshua."[5] Stern's conclusion is that the case can and should be made for using the subjective genitive case in Rom 3:22 and elsewhere in the Pauline letters. In other words, Rom 3:22 is where "the rubber meets the road."

In expanding the study beyond Stern's commentary, I have learned that at least as far back as the nineteenth century, a forceful minority has advocated the subjective position.

In Paul's Greek usage, is Christ delivering or receiving the action? If the subjective genitive translation is correct, then Christ is the subject, and it is the infinite faith of Christ alone that delivers the atonement, overcomes sin, and provides justification for the sinner. However, if the objective genitive translation is correct, then Christ is the object receiving the finite faith that the believer is contributing to his or her own salvation.

I am arguing that Christ is the *subject* and that his atonement *delivers* the benefit that overcomes human sin—If Christ is the sole connection between God's perfection and humanity's imperfection then it follows that salvation is the result of the Son's atonement and the Father's forgiveness. God-as-Son provides the affirmative action that "overcomes" human sin and "justifies" the forgiveness that comes from God-as-Father.

---

4. Ibid., 348.
5. Stern, *Jewish New Testament Commentary*, 347, 538.

The believer, on the other hand, is the *object* who *receives* the benefit of Christ's atonement. Obviously, having "faith in Jesus Christ" is an important aspect on life's journey, but it is derivative rather than salvific. That is, salvation is derived from the infinite "faith [or faithfulness] *of* Jesus Christ," rather than the finite faith of the believer.

Paul's indictment against human nature in Rom 3:23 ("all have sinned") and Rom 6:23 ("the wages of sin is death) further confirms that Jesus is the *subject* causing the action and the sinner is the *object* receiving the benefit. In other words, salvation is based on Christ's faithfulness in going to the cross for sin, rather than on my faithfulness in believing that he went to the cross for sin.

The contrast between the typical handshake and a Roman forearm handshake illustrates the difference between finite faith and the infinite faithfulness of Christ. With the traditional handshake, the grip is palm-to-palm, and if one loses his grip, the connection is broken. However, with the Roman handshake, each person grasps the other person's wrist, and the connection remains even if one person loses his grip. My salvation, therefore, is based upon the fact that Christ is holding onto me rather than the idea that I am holding onto Christ.

MODERN USE OF OBJECTIVE GENITIVE

So how do we account for the widespread use of the objective case that is seen in so many English translations? By way of background, we can say that the *King James Version* of the Bible was the "gold standard" for many years. It is a "word-for-word" English translation that dates back to 1611. A few English translations were published near the beginning of the twentieth century, including *The Revised Version* of the King James in 1885 (RV), and the *American Standard Version in* 1901 (ASV).

However, a noticeable increase of English translations occurred in the last half of the twentieth century as Westerners began to focus more and more on the significance of the individual. The process of "updating" the Bible began in earnest as word-for-word translations tried to develop a more readable style. These projects included *The Revised Standard Version* in 1952 and 1989 (RSV, NRSV), the *New American Standard Bible* in 1971 and 1995 (NASB), and the *New King James Version* in 1982 (NKJV).

These word-for-word projects were followed by "thought-for-thought" projects that sought further readability. This new process, usually referred to as dynamic equivalence, included the *New English Bible* in 1970 and 1989 (NEB and REB), the *New International Version* in 1978, 1996, 1996, and 2005 (NIV, NIRV, NIVI, TNIV), and the *Holman Christian Standard Bible* in 2004 (HCSB).

But there was a continuing demand for a Bible that was even more reader-friendly. A number of scholars responded with "paraphrased" versions that were more readable but less literal, such as *The Living Bible* in 1971 (TLB), the *Good News Bible* in 1976 (GNB), the *New Living Translation* in 1996 (NLT), and *The Message* in 2002 (MSG). And in 2011 there was *The Kingdom New Testament* (KNT) which is allegedly a "new translation" in everyday speech."[6]

Determining the reason for the transition from the subjective genitive in the seventeenth century to the objective genitive in the twentieth century translations is beyond the scope of this study. However, even a cursory acquaintance with European and American history would suggest that the biblical transition is somehow related to the philosophical and cultural transition from the premodern era to the modern/postmodern era. One aspect of this seismic shift in Western civilization has been the drift away from the "other-worldliness" of the premodern era toward the modern/postmodern emphasis on "this-world." The modern era has led to a wide-ranging pluralism where the Judeo-Christian tradition has had to compete with not only established world religions, but also new spiritualities, including New Age mysticisms and various forms of secular humanism.

The transition from subjective genitive to objective genitive may also have a religious connotation, particularly as it relates to the Protestant Reformation and the political upheaval that followed. The Protestant movement was augmented by the development of the printing press and other forms of science and technology. The new developments challenged traditional authority by focusing on the individual and his or her capacity to bring about change in the temporal world. These new "Protestants" denied the universal authority of the Roman Catholic Church and entrusted greater authority to the individual. Indeed, the "priesthood of the believer" and "justification by faith" became rallying cries that pitted the

---

6. Gundry, "Tom's Targum," para. 4.

Faith of Jesus Christ

conscience of the individual believer against the collective authority of the Catholic Church.

New questions regarding the nature of salvation eventually led to an intramural contest between Calvinism and Arminianism as the two sides argued over the role of the individual in salvation. Calvinists understood the sovereignty of God to mean that God had "elected" or "predestined" certain individuals for salvation and drawn them to himself through faith alone. Rejecting Calvin's understanding of "predestination," the Arminians held that Christ's atonement was available to anyone who put his or her faith in Christ.

Theological issues regarding justification (being made right with God) and the nature of personal salvation have been hotly debated throughout the five hundred years that have lapsed since the Sixteenth Century Reformation. And they continue today as seen in the controversy between present day stalwarts N.T. Wright and John Piper. Piper's book *The Future of Justification: A Response to N.T. Wright* (2007) fired a new volley in response to Wright's work, and Wright's book *Justification: God's Plan and Paul's Vision* (2009) fired back. So how are these issues related to the problem of subjective genitive vs. objective genitive?

A PROBLEM AND THE SOLUTION

At its most basic level, Paul's letter to the church in Rome presents both the *problem* and a *solution*. As mentioned earlier, from Rom 1:1 through Rom 3:20, Paul explained that personal accountability for sin is humanity's ultimate problem. Then from Rom 3:21 through Rom 16:27, he presented the good news that Jesus Christ was and is the solution to the problem.

Rom 3:21–22 is the decisive point in the Book of Romans because it is the point of transition from the problem to the solution. Indeed, the apostle used the phrase *dia pisteos Iesou Christou* ("by faith of Jesus Christ") like a pivot to move from the problem to the solution. Imagine that a football player is moving down the field in one direction when he suddenly sets one foot, pivots, and begins moving in a new direction. Similarly, having established the incompatibility that exists between the righteousness of God and sinful humanity, Paul "sets his foot," pivots, and begins explaining that there is now a *new manifestation* of the righteousness of God. This new manifestation is to benefit all of humanity, and especially "those who believe."

Paul explained the "faith of Jesus Christ" as the ultimate manifestation of divine righteousness, something that is totally "apart from the Law." We know the apostle used the phrase—*dia pisteos Iesou Christou*—to communicate a key doctrine, because he used the same Greek construction in Rom 3:26, twice in Gal 2:16, 3:22, in Eph 3:12, and in Phil 3:9. Stern says the apostle also used a similar construction in Col 2:12 and 2 Thess 2:13.[7]

It is interesting to study Paul's progression as he moves from accountability as the problem to redemption as the solution. As any good communicator would do, Paul began with a theme that was familiar to his audience and moved on to something that was entirely new. He began with the righteousness of God that had been "witnessed" by the law and the prophets in the Old Testament, and then moved to the New Testament experience. The righteousness of God has "now" been "manifested" in a new way—that is, "through the faith of Jesus Christ" (Rom 3:21–22 KJV).

Notice how the "righteousness of God" progresses from God, through Christ, to humankind within Rom 3:21–23 KJV:

> 1) What? The preexisting *"righteousness of God"* is separate and "apart from the Law" (v.21a).
>
> 2) When? Though previously "witnessed by the Law and the Prophets," *now* apart from the law, the "righteousness of God has been manifested" in a new way (v.21b).
>
> 3) How? This "righteousness of God" has now been manifested *through the faith of Jesus Christ* (v. 22a).
>
> 4) For Whom? ". . . for *all* those who believe." Furthermore, "there is no distinction" among those who believe (v.22b).
>
> 5) Why? "For *all have sinned* and come short of the glory of God" (v.23).

In Rom 3:21, 22, and 23, the power of God flows earthward almost like gravity causes water to flow down the side of a mountain. Paul starts v.21 with the infinite "righteousness of God" [God-as-Father]. This "righteousness" enters the finite realm of time and space in the person of Jesus Christ [God-as-Son]. Having entered the temporal world and having

---

7. Ibid., 347.

"humbled Himself by becoming obedient to the point of death, even death on a cross" (Phil 2:8), Christ overcomes sin and death by his resurrection from the dead. And through his faithfulness *(by faith of Jesus Christ,)* the benefits of divine forgiveness flow on down to the finite inhabitants of the world, "for all those who believe" (v.22b).

The idea that the apostle would use the objective genitive to insert human action at the very beginning of his exposition of God's plan of redemption seems strangely out of place. I would argue, instead, that it is more likely that Paul's statement regarding the "faith *of* Jesus Christ" relegates believers to a position of being beneficiaries of the amazing grace that comes to humankind via the faithfulness of Christ.

So what is the explanation for the massive use of the objective genitive in modern translations of the Bible? I am not a historian, but I would suggest that the answer is somehow bound up in the previously discussed transition from the "other-worldliness" of the medieval era to modernity's focus on "this world." We know, for example, that beginning with the Renaissance in the fourteenth century, the modern era has focused on the individual in disciplines like philosophy, literature, and the arts. The contrast becomes visual in the history of architecture where Western civilization moves from the Gothic cathedrals built to glorify God to modern buildings that emphasize human functionality.

The same phenomenon is seen in the transition from the Roman Catholic hegemony to the schism that produced the Protestant Reformation in the sixteenth century. In former times, the church served as the spiritual gatekeeper that monitored individual spirituality. Education was limited, and most parishioners could not read the Bible much less study the profound message of the gospel. Fueled by the invention of moveable type and new printing presses, the Protestant Reformation opened the floodgates and shifted the focus from the collective authority of the Catholic Church to the Protestant tradition where the individual assumes the role of spiritual gatekeeper.

The expanded use of the objective genitive in modern translations of the Bible may have benefited from the Reformation's emphasis on the individual. As a Protestant, I would say the upside of the Reformation was to emphasize the importance of having a personal relationship with God through Jesus Christ—instead of relying on the collective authority of the Roman Catholic Church.

Christianity and the Outsider

However, the downside is that over the years the Protestant tradition has overemphasized the importance of the individual. Unfortunately, individual spirituality seems to have evolved into a "religious individualism" where the individual not only receives the gift of eternal life through Jesus Christ (Rom 6:23) but also plays an active role in obtaining the gift—That is, the individual allegedly comes into right relationship with God by deliberately putting his or her "faith in Jesus Christ" as previously discussed in the objective genitive interpretation of Rom 3:22.

In summary, I would argue that the subjective genitive translation (faith *of* Jesus Christ) is more accurate than the objective genitive translation (faith *in* Jesus Christ) for the following reasons:

First, the apostle Paul opened the Book of Romans by establishing humanity's general accountability to God. On one hand, Paul laid the groundwork for the subjective genitive interpretation by focusing on humanity's universal accountability for sin. General accountability is spread throughout chapters 1 and 2, as well as the first part of chapter 3. As if to further accentuate the point, Paul closed the section on accountability by quoting Psalms 14: "There is none righteous, not even one; There is none who understands, There is none who seeks for God . . . There is no fear of God before their eyes" (Rom 3:10–11, 18).

Rom 3:20 finalizes the sin problem with the statement that even "the knowledge of sin" comes through the accountability of the law. There is no hint that in the next two verses, human faith is going to help solve the sin problem by having "faith in Jesus Christ," no groundwork for an objective genitive interpretation that would justify the abrupt appearance of having "faith in Jesus Christ, and nothing suggests that these sinful people should suddenly be assigned a role in manifesting the righteousness of God though *their* "faith in Jesus Christ" (Rom 3:21–22).

Second, in Rom 3:21–22, we see that the Law and the Prophets *"witnessed"* the "righteousness of God," but they were not *part of* the manifestation of that righteousness. By the same token, the followers of Jesus Christ are *"witnesses"* to the "righteousness of God," but we are not *part of* the manifestation of that righteousness. Christ alone is the manifestation of the "righteousness of God."

With the subjective genitive, Paul declares that the "righteousness of God" has been manifested on earth and then explains how it had been manifested, that is, *dia pisteos*—"through faith *of*" Jesus Christ. The objective genitive, on the other hand, would have Paul interjecting the faith of each individual at the very beginning of the redemptive process. That is, the "righteousness of God" would have been manifested by calling upon the finite faith of human beings who have somehow intervened in God's manifestation process by virtue of having personal "faith in Jesus Christ."

The subjective genitive correctly acknowledges that the *infinite* "faith of Jesus Christ" is the catalyst of salvation, leaving each person's *finite* "faith in Jesus Christ" as a derivative or a by-product of the faithfulness of Jesus, himself. In other words, the objective genitive interpretation misconstrues the "manifestation" of the "righteousness of God" by introducing human faith too early.

Third, the "righteousness of God" is *actively* manifested "through the faith *of* Jesus Christ" (KJV) and then *passively* received by the sinner—"for all have sinned and come short of the glory of God" (Rom 3:23). The sinner is receiving grace rather than assisting in its manifestation. The subjective genitive confirms the salvific flow of forgiveness. It is an *earthward* flow from the infinite Father, through the infinite Son, to finite human beings who benefit from the atonement of the Son. Every reference to humanity in Rom 3:21–31 leaves human beings on the passive or receiving end of salvation, except for the questionable use of the objective genitive in Rom 3:22 where the believer allegedly puts his finite "faith in Jesus Christ." In other words, finite faith "in Christ" enters the Rom 3:21–22 scenario only through the translator's use of the objective genitive case.

All of the above references reflect the imperfect or "fallen" state of humankind. To suggest that "fallen" men and women can actively assist in their own salvation by placing their faith in Christ is to suppose that one can overcome the law of gravity by "falling up" or lifting himself by pulling on his own bootstraps. Having spelled out human accountability from Rom 1:1 through Rom 3:20, Paul used Rom 3:21–31 to confirm that Christ alone is the manifestation of divine righteousness. The finite sinner is then "justified as a gift *by* His [the Father's] grace *through* the redemption which is *in* Christ Jesus [the Son] (v. 24).

If the "faith *of* Jesus Christ" alone is salvific, rather than an individual having "faith *in* Jesus Christ," then where does the human perspective fit into the gospel story? Having discussed the infinite "faith of Jesus Christ" in the previous section, we now turn to the finite idea of "repentance toward God."

Christianity and the Outsider

REPENTANCE: THE HUMAN ASPECT

A few years ago newspapers reported that a defective door had broken loose on a highflying aircraft causing it to lose cabin pressure. Because the pressure inside the cabin was higher than on the outside, there was a sudden decompression. Everything that was not tied down was sucked out the door of the aircraft—Newspapers and books, hats and coats, and even people were suddenly gone! The possibility of decompression is the reason airline passengers are encouraged to keep their seatbelts loosely fastened at all times.

As I read the news story, it occurred to me that physical decompression in an aircraft is similar to the spiritual decompression that occurs when a person repents of what C. S. Lewis called an "anti-God state of mind."[8] Repentance means that a person has experienced a radical change of direction—like a drill sergeant shouting "to the rear, march." The apostle Paul said the "stubbornness and unrepentant heart" of the "natural man" is gone (Rom 2:5, 1 Cor 2:12), and the "spiritual man" receives "the Spirit who is from God . . . (1 Cor 2:12a, 15).

Repentance involves a passive humbling of self, rather than claiming an active role in the redemptive process. While repentance will be discussed more fully in chapter 18, the point here is merely to show repentance as a "condition precedent."

Repentance *does not cause redemption*, but it must come *before redemption*. Repentance is similar to a "condition precedent" in a real estate transaction. For example, both buyer and seller may have signed a written document, and the deal may look final. However, if the document has a clause that says the deal is subject to the approval of the buyer's attorney then the document is not a binding contract. No approval! No contract! Legally, the attorney's approval is not part of the transaction, but it is a condition precedent to the transaction—It must occur before there is a binding agreement for the transaction to move forward.

Spiritually speaking, personal repentance has no part in redemption, but it must occur before the redemptive process will move forward. The apostle Paul said "the kindness of God leads you to repentance" (Rom 2:4). That is, God "draws," or "entices" sinners toward repentance, but he will not force repentance upon an unrepentant heart (Rom 2:5). No repentance! No redemptive process! Before repentance, the physical heart

---

8. Lewis, *Mere Christianity*, 122.

is beating, but the person is spiritually dead. "The wages of sin is death" (Rom 6:23a). However, when the repentant heart is emptied before God, the Son's atonement and the Father's forgiveness enter like air pressure entering a vacuum. In other words, the sinner receives eternal life solely through the faithfulness *of* Jesus Christ and the resulting forgiveness that is available through the grace of God (Rom 6:23b, Rom 3:22).

Faith in Christ, on the other hand, depends upon a person having knowledge of the new covenant and acting on that knowledge. Theologically, a person's finite "faith *in* Christ" is derivative; that is, it results from the infinite "faith *of* Christ." As the apostle said, "Now we [Christians] have received . . . the Spirit who is from God, that we might *know* the things freely given to us by God" (1 Cor 2:12b). After all, how could one have faith in an object of which he is unaware? In other words, how can a person have faith in Jesus Christ if he is unaware of Christ and his atonement for sin?

Paul addressed the issue of knowledge in connection with Israel's rejection of the Messiah in Romans 9 through 11. Paul ran the gauntlet of calling, believing, hearing, and preaching and then said, "So then faith cometh by hearing, and hearing by the word *(rema)* of God" (Rom 10:17 KJV). *Rema* is the spoken or uttered word of God rather than the eternal Word *(logos)*—that is, Jesus Christ who is the pre-incarnate Word of God. Paul then asked and immediately answered a rhetorical question, "But I say, Have they not heard? Yes verily, their sound went into *all* the earth, and their words *(rema)* unto the *ends of the earth*" (Rom 10:18). The apostle goes on to quote Moses and Isaiah to show that this *rema* has been "uttered" in a way that creates divine accountability not only for Israel and the church but also for the rest of the world (Rom 10:18–21 KJV).

In the fourth gospel, Jesus specifically addressed the question of knowledge when he said, "And if anyone hears My sayings *(rema),* and does not keep them, I do not judge him; for I did not come to judge the world, but to save the world. He who rejects Me, and does not receive My sayings *(rema),* has one who judges him; the word *(logos)* I spoke is what will judge him *in the last day*" (John 12:47–48). John seems to be saying that eternal judgment is not determined solely by a person's awareness of and response to the words or sayings *(rema)* of the new covenant, but by the perfect justice of the eternal *logos* that will judge all people "in the last day."

Continuing the previous contract illustration, having "faith in Christ" is more like a "condition subsequent" in a real estate contract. That is, a clause in the contract can refer to something that might happen *after* the agreement becomes binding. With a typical real estate transaction, the contract is completed and ownership of the property is transferred to the buyer. However, under the original terms of the contract, the new owner's rights can be subjected to restrictions in the deed that continue to apply after the deal is consummated. For example, the use of the property may be limited to a particular purpose, like a church or a park, and a subsequent violation of the restriction can bring severe consequences to the owner who violates the restrictions.

On one hand, personal repentance before God occurs *before* redemption, and it has no part in bringing about redemption. On the other hand, true faith in Christ occurs *after* redemption. Of course, for the insiders who are privy to the new covenant, true repentance and authentic faith are so closely associated that they may seem to occur simultaneously.

Unfortunately, it is also possible for a person to confess his or her "faith in Christ" without having experienced true repentance. Indeed, Christian churches are full of people who have confessed their faith in Christ, but they go on living as if nothing has happened.

I would argue, however, that a person cannot repent of his "anti-God state of mind" without being a changed person. When the finite will is neutralized, the infinite will of God does the work of justification through the faithfulness of Christ. The Son's death on the cross pays the price for sin, justifies the sinner, and opens the door to the Father's forgiveness. Like a jet engine lifting an aircraft, the faithfulness of Christ is the power that "lifts" the burden of sin and cleanses the sinner from all unrighteousness. Figuratively speaking, it is Christ who does the "heavy lifting."

When the repentant sinner is emptied of self sufficiency, the pride of self-importance is done away with, and the grace of God does the rest. Seamlessly, the Son's atonement justifies and the Father's grace forgives the sinner. No one really understands God's amazing grace and how spiritual decompression works, yet a repentant person can say with the blind man, ". . . one thing I know, that, whereas I was blind, now I see" (John 9:25).

I am a "stiff upper-lip" kind of person who always tries to control his emotions. But a few years ago, I was forced to confront a situation that was especially painful. Throughout the ordeal I had acted professionally and maintained self-control. However, as I walked into a particular meeting, two friends approached me and offered their support. Suddenly, my emotions boiled over. I lost all composure and cried like a baby! Repentance is not mere emotion, but it is similar to the uncontrollable welling up of one's emotions. It is a spiritual implosion that challenges the ultimate meaning of one's existence. Realizing that one is nothing in comparison to God brings total submission to the God of the universe. So what's the difference between repentance and faith?

As mentioned earlier, what God knows about us is more important than what we know about God. The fact that a covenant insider "knows" enough to have "faith in Jesus Christ" is a significant part of sanctification and what Jesus called the abundant life. But knowledge, as such, is not salvific. Indeed, a salvation that is somehow conditioned upon human knowledge, including the knowledge required in order to have "faith in Christ," is somehow reminiscent of the teachings of the ancient Gnostics who allegedly possessed secret knowledge as well as the special privileges that went along with that knowledge.

Jesus' closing message in Luke's gospel says ". . . repentance for forgiveness of sins should be proclaimed in His name to all nations, beginning in Jerusalem" (Luke 24:47). But *why* does the grace of God make forgiveness available, and *how* does it happen?

12

Forgiveness: The Why and the How

Why should an infinite, perfect God forgive finite, imperfect human beings for their sinful imperfection? And if forgiveness is somehow available through Jesus Christ, how can his crucifixion in Jerusalem two thousand years ago have universal significance for people hundreds and even thousands of years before and after the cross?

THE NATURE OF FORGIVENESS

The apostle Paul urged people to forgive each other ". . . just as God in Christ also has forgiven *(charizomai)* you" (Eph 4:32). Paul's choice of the word *charizomai* or "graciously forgiven" is particularly significant because it focuses attention on the nature of grace *(charis)* rather than on the person receiving grace. The *act* of forgiving, as opposed to *receiving* forgiveness, reveals the grace of God and serves as an exemplar for human behavior. It spotlights the God of the second chance who forgives our unrighteousness and provides a model for the father who forgives his rebellious child, or the wife who forgives her unfaithful husband.

Forgiveness is the reverse side of accountability. Whereas divine justice makes us accountable for sin, divine grace provides forgiveness from sin. Divine justice puts human imperfection at risk, but divine forgiveness bridges the gulf between divine perfection and human imperfection.

Forgiveness: The Why and the How

Forgiveness is a continuing picture that unfolds throughout the Bible. The human predicament is like the criminal defense lawyer who said his clients did not want "justice"—They wanted "off"! Humanly speaking, we don't want justice—We want forgiveness! The prophet Hosea is a wonderful example of forgiveness; he repeatedly forgave his wife for her unfaithfulness. Through God's grace, Hosea saw Gomer's unfaithfulness to her husband as a picture of Israel's unfaithfulness to God: "*Return, O Israel, to the Lord your God . . . I will heal their apostasy, I will love them freely*" (Hos 14:1, 4). In Luke's story of the prodigal son, we see both the *repentance* of the son and the forgiveness of the father (Luke 15:11–32). In the life and work of the apostle Paul, we see forgiveness within the church when he says "And be kind to one another, tender-hearted, forgiving *(charizomai)* each other, just as God in Christ also has forgiven *(charizomai)* you" (Eph 4:32).

However, when the focus shifts from the forgiver to the person who needs forgiveness, then Paul's word choice shifts from *charizomai* to either *paresis* (pass by) or *aphesis* (cancel or send away). We will study the difference between *paresis* and *aphesis* in the next chapter. However, having confirmed that all people have sinned (Rom 3:23), that all people need forgiveness (Rom 6:23), and that God's grace is sufficient (Rom 5:20–21), we can now discuss *why* forgiveness is available and *how* guilty people can be forgiven.

FORGIVENESS: THE FIRST QUESTION—WHY

Why should a guilty defendant be exonerated? Something is supposed to happen in a courtroom when a guilty verdict is announced. The guilty party can be fined, placed on probation, incarcerated, or even executed, but he cannot walk away as if nothing has happened! There is accountability in a courtroom even when the technical plea of "no contest" is entered. Divine perfection requires perfect justice, and perfect justice is on a collision course with humanity's sinful imperfection.

The apostle Paul began Romans with a proclamation of human guilt—"For the wrath of God is revealed from heaven against all ungodliness and unrighteousness of men, who suppress the truth in unrighteousness" (Rom 1:18). Spread out over the first two and a half chapters of Romans, the indictment charges that the whole world is "accountable to

God ... for through the Law comes the knowledge of sin (Rom 3:19–20). Perfect justice requires the determination of guilt and the carrying out of the sentence.

However, in Rom 3:21, the apostle begins to explain *why* some guilty sinners are to be exonerated. They must be exonerated because perfect justice also requires the release of a defendant when the penalty has been satisfied. In a court case, for example, if the judgment is that the defendant must pay a $100 fine, then the case is closed when the fine is paid—*even if someone else pays the fine*. Having established universal guilt, the apostle begins to explain that someone has already paid the price and arranged a satisfaction of judgment.

Perfect justice meets *the gift of grace* in Rom 3:24! Paul explains that God's perfect grace, in the person of Jesus Christ, intervened on behalf of sinful humanity and satisfied the requirements of perfect justice. In other words, sinful people are cleared or "justified" by the "grace-work" of Jesus Christ.

So what is this "grace-work" all about? On one hand, God has a zero-tolerance for sinful imperfection, but on the other hand, he is in the business of reclaiming sinful imperfection. Strictly speaking, the situation defies human understanding. It is as if a parent's childcare strategy uses one tactic with the right hand and an opposing tactic with the left hand—simultaneously chastising with one hand and caressing with the other.

In Greek, *lutron* means "ransom." It was the price required to redeem a person out of slavery. Even in contemporary kidnapping cases, parents sometimes pay a ransom for the release of a child. Not surprisingly, *lutron* is the root word in the term Paul used to explain "the redemption (*apolutrosis*) that is in Christ Jesus" (Rom 3:24). Paul used the purchase of a person out of slavery to dramatize the redemption of a sinner out of sin.

Biblically speaking, the Father's "perfect justice" required that a price be paid for humanity's sinful imperfection, and the Son's "perfect love" paid the price. Each person is a "slave to sin." Therefore, the sin problem could be solved only if the necessary price were paid to remove people from sin. In other words, the Father's perfection required justice, and on the cross the Son's perfection paid the "ransom" to obtain each sinner's release from his or her slavery to sin (Rom 6:6, 16–23).

Forgiveness: The Why and the How

Justice or Love, or Both

The contrast between God's *justice* and his *love* seems to leave us with a paradoxical situation. However, there is a divine strategy at work in the Christ event, and it produces a unity of purpose. As the prophet Isaiah said, "Let every valley be lifted up, And every mountain and hill be made low; And let the rough ground become a plain, Then the glory of the Lord will be revealed, And all flesh will see it together, For the mouth of the Lord has spoken" (Isa 40:4–5).

The Christ event transforms the high road of justice and the low road of sin into God's "glory road." The scenario is as if the judge in a criminal case has rendered a just decision against a guilty defendant. Ordinarily, the defendant would be handcuffed and led away to prison. But, let us suppose that the law allows a judge to free the defendant if someone else is willing to serve the defendant's sentence. The "substitution" would allow the judge to enter a just sentence and then volunteer to serve the sentence, himself. At that point, he would remove his robe and descend from the bench. He would then be handcuffed and led off to prison—taking the defendant's punishment upon himself.

Perfect justice made every human being a debtor, but *perfect love* paid the debt. Christ's atonement provided the payment, and his resurrection provided the proof of payment—an inglorious *payment* followed by a glorious *proof of payment*. No wonder the apostle Paul said, "But if there is no resurrection of the dead, not even Christ has been raised; and if Christ has not been raised, then our preaching is vain, your faith also is vain" (1 Cor 15:13–14).

In the eyes of the law, the release of a defendant who has served his sentence or paid his fine is not a matter of mercy. Justice, itself, requires that an inmate be released when his or her "debt to society" has been paid. Indeed, the payment of a fine satisfies the law even if an innocent third party pays the fine. Continuing the earlier analogy, God's right-handed justice (God-as-Father) required human accountability for sin, but his left-handed compassion (God-as-Son) paid the price for humanity's sinful unrighteousness and opened the door to the Father's forgiveness.

Christianity and the Outsider

Linking Forgiveness and Repentance

The Father's forgiveness is linked to the crucifixion of the Son, then the crucifixion is linked back to the animal sacrifices that had been occurring in Israel's sacrificial system—a system in which the "price" for sin was paid symbolically in the blood of an unblemished animal. From Abel's acceptable sacrifice, to Israel's sacrificial system, to the crucifixion of Christ, ". . . without shedding of blood there is no forgiveness" (Heb 9:22).

Divine forgiveness was a matter of life and death for Jesus, and spiritually speaking, it's a matter of life and death for every individual. The writer of Hebrews used a Last Will and Testament to illustrate the life and death nature of God's forgiveness. A person's will doesn't take effect until his or her death. The law says a will is ambulatory, meaning that it "walks" along with the maker or "testator" until death occurs. As the writer of Hebrews said, "For where a covenant [Last Will] is, there must of necessity be the death of the one who made it. For a covenant is valid only when men are dead, for it is never in force while the one who made it lives" (Heb 9:16–17). In other words, the death of Jesus Christ provides forgiveness for repentant sinners, just as the death of the testator effectuates a gift to a beneficiary in a will. However, the significance of the cross is not limited to the suffering and dying.

The ultimate meaning of the cross is that Christ suffered and died for a cosmic purpose—that is, to make atonement for the sinful imperfection of the world. As the apostle Paul said, the grace of God is manifested "through the redemption which is in Christ Jesus" (Rom 3:24). Like a mother using a sponge to wipe away spilled milk, Christ's atonement washes away sin and purifies the broken and contrite heart.

However, is divine grace retail or wholesale? Is God's grace discounted so as to provide wholesale forgiveness for everybody? Or is forgiveness retailed in the sense that it is available only on an individual basis and at full price? The Bible says divine forgiveness is linked to the sin of each individual and that God paid the supreme price when "He gave his only begotten Son."

But how is forgiveness individualized? The closing passage of Luke's gospel identifies *repentance* (the broken and contrite heart) as the linkage between individual accountability and divine forgiveness. Given in the form of marching orders to his followers, Jesus said ". . . *repentance* for *forgiveness* of sins should be proclaimed in His name to all the nations, beginning from Jerusalem " (Luke 24:47).

We refer to the Easter story as "the passion of Christ" because he gave the last full measure of his earthly sojourn to atone for the sin of the world. Of course, human mortality means that all people will eventually experience the "passion" of physical death. But a person must also experience the "passion" of spiritual death in the sense that repentance causes one to die to self. The apostle Paul said, "I am crucified with Christ; nevertheless I live" (Gal 2:20 KJV). The surrender of self is not the casual religiosity that is implied in the idea of wholesale grace. Dietrich Bonhoeffer's (1906–1945) famous reference to "cheap grace" says it all; "... cheap grace is the preaching of forgiveness without requiring repentance."[1]

In view of the biblical record, it would be scandalous for anyone to identify divine forgiveness with the casual "justice" meted out by judges who have allowed their courtrooms to become turnstiles of "injustice" where the guilty return time after time making a mockery of justice. The same principle applies to weak parents who threaten their children with discipline, but fail to hold them accountable for bad behavior. They love their children, but their inconsistency causes the children to develop into unruly youngsters and dysfunctional adults.

Paul said God's forgiveness was consummated "... in Christ Jesus whom God displayed publicly as a propitiation (*hilasterion*) in his blood ..." (Rom 3:25). *Hilasterion* is a term used only twice in the New Testament: as "propitiation" in Rom 3:25 and as "mercy seat" in Heb 9:5. The apostle used *hilasterion* in order to revisit Hebrew history where the "mercy seat" was the "lid" that covered the sacred Ark of the Covenant—(the same "Ark" that made Harrison Ford a movie star in *Raiders of the Lost Ark*). In Hebrew tradition, the Day of Atonement *(Yom Kippur)* was the "time" and the mercy seat was the "place" where the high priest sprinkled the blood of a sacrificial animal as a symbolic "payment" for the sins of the people.

The apostle Paul identified Jesus, himself, as the *hilasterion*—the sacrificial "payment" for the sins of the people. The apostle was not only pointing out that a unique sacrifice had taken place on the cross, but also confirming that the old symbolism had been left behind forever. In former times, the high priest offered a symbolic sacrifice. That is, he sprinkled the

---

1. Bonhoeffer, *The Cost of Discipleship*, 36.

death-blood of an animal on the "mercy seat" as a symbolic payment for the sins of Israel. However, the Christ event means that it was the death-blood of "God with us" that was shed on the cross.

The crucified Christ was the *ultimate mercy seat* because his own blood was poured out as a payment for the sinful imperfection of humankind. Through the mystery of the Trinity, God required the sacrifice, and God, in Christ, was the sacrifice that was offered. On the cross, the "who, what, when, where, and why" of Israel's sacrificial system were eliminated, and Jesus, himself, fulfilled those requirements with a once-for-all-time sacrifice:

> Jesus was the high priest *who* administered the blood sacrifice.
> His blood was *what* was sacrificed.
> His crucifixion was the time *when* the sacrifice was made.
> His cross was the place *where* the sacrifice was made.
> And *why* was the sacrifice made? Because ". . . God so loved the world that He gave His only begotten Son . . . " (John 3:16).

Perfection Meets Imperfection

The Christ event was the intersection between heaven's perfection and earth's imperfection. *Perfect justice* required a final judgment as well as a satisfaction of the judgment—And Jesus was the medium of satisfaction. *Perfect love* required forgiveness—And Jesus was the medium of divine forgiveness. Human imperfection created the debt, and God-as-Son paid the debt. "Greater love has no one than this, that one lay down his life for his friends" (John 15:13).

It should also be noted that Israel's sacrificial system required the *very best* as the medium of sacrifice. The Law of Moses required that a "lamb without blemish" be used in sacrificial offerings. We now realize that the sacrifice of a lamb *without blemish* was symbolic of ". . . the blood of Christ, who through the eternal Spirit offered Himself *without blemish*" (Heb 9:14).

The "high road" of Jewish tradition provides a sharp contrast to the "low road" of Greek tradition, which Jacques Derrida described in "Plato's Pharmacy." Whereas Israel's sacrificial system used an animal without blemish to foreshadow the atonement of a redeemer without blemish, "The Athenians regularly maintained a number of degraded and useless beings at the public expense; and when any calamity, such as plague, drought, or famine, befell the city, they sacrificed two of these outcasts as scapegoats."[2] The practice was to appease the gods with purification rituals. However, instead of offering a "lamb without blemish," they selected from among themselves a fellow citizen who was sickly, deformed, or otherwise of no use to them. They wanted to appease the divine anger that had supposedly brought storms and pestilence to their city, but chose to use a medium that cost them very little.

FORGIVENESS: THE SECOND QUESTION—HOW

How can the crucifixion of Jesus Christ at a particular place and a particular time (space/time) be understood to have universal significance for people who lived hundreds or even thousands of years either *before* or *after* the Cross?

Historically, the Christ event has played a major role in the development of Western civilization. Those of us who are part of the Judeo-Christian tradition understand ourselves to be beneficiaries of God's "special revelation." But, whether one speaks of special revelation in terms of Israel's original covenant or Christianity's new covenant (Luke 22:20, 2 Cor 3:6, Heb 8:8, 13:24), we must acknowledge that extraordinary consequences flow from the idea of special revelation. To have been born Jewish instead of Hindu would certainly give one an advantage in the context of God's special relationship with Israel. Similarly, being born in the so-called Christian West instead of Sub-Sahara Africa gives one an obvious advantage in terms of putting one's faith in Jesus Christ.

Privity of Contract

Perhaps it will help us understand the nature of divine covenants by discussing them in relationship to the law of contracts. A contract comes into existence when a valid "offer" is made by one party and "accepted" by a second party. With this meeting of the minds, the people who entered into the contract are said to have "privity of contract" with each other. That is, there is a direct connection between the contracting parties. We say the party of the first part and the party of the second part are "privy"

2. Derrida, "Plato's Pharmacy," 133.

Christianity and the Outsider

to the contract and that outside third parties are "not privy" to the contract. "Privy" or "privity" comes from the Latin word *privatus* and refers to private or special knowledge, including one's participation in such knowledge. Simply stated, some people are included under the terms of the contract, and everyone else is excluded!

Some people will be offended by the very idea of human beings entering into a contract with God—and rightly so. No one can make a "deal" with God. It would be ludicrous to think that God would negotiate with humankind. It is especially ridiculous to think of God entering into a bilateral contract as if a "promise for a promise" were being negotiated between equal parties.

Unilateral Contracts

It might be helpful, however, to use the idea of a unilateral contract in order to illustrate certain aspects of the biblical covenants—as long as one realizes that mere participation in the covenant is not salvific. Membership by virtue of being born into a group or later joining the group does not guarantee salvation.

Whereas a typical contract is bilateral, that is, a *"promise for a promise,"* a unilateral contract is a *"promise for an act."* The offer of a reward is a classic example of a unilateral contract. For example, if someone offers a sum of money in exchange for the return of a pet, then another person's promise to return the pet is of no consequence. Only the *act* of returning the animal will consummate the arrangement.

It seems to me that the idea of God's unilateral "promise" and Abraham's responsive "act" might be useful in exploring the nature of God's covenant relationship with Israel. Regarding the covenant with Israel, the Bible says, "Now the Lord said to Abram, Go forth from your country . . . To the land which I will show you; And I will make you a great nation, And I will bless you, And make your name great; And so you shall be a blessing; And I will bless those who bless you, And the one who curses you I will curse, And in you all the families of the earth shall be blessed" (Gen 12:1–3). The Lord did not negotiate with Abram, but he did make a promise that was conditioned upon Abraham's obedience.

The very next verse says, "So Abram went forth as the Lord had spoken to him . . . " (Gen 12:4). In other words, Abram *obeyed* God! As the writer of Hebrews would later write, "By faith Abraham, when he was called, *obeyed* by going out to a place which he was to receive for an inheritance; and he went out, not knowing where he was going. By faith he lived as an alien in the land of promise, a foreign land, dwelling in tents with Isaac and Jacob, fellow-heirs of the same promise; for he was looking for the city which has foundations, whose architect and builder is God" (Heb 11:8–10).

While no illustration can adequately explain the nature of special revelation, I would argue that the idea of a "promise for an act" is a viable approximation of God's special revelation to Israel and eventually to the rest of the world. Whether one speaks of the earlier "covenant" with Israel or the "new covenant" in Christ, the Judeo-Christian tradition teaches that each group played a role in God's ultimate plan of salvation.

Part IV
*Special Revelation:
Life Within a Covenant*

———————

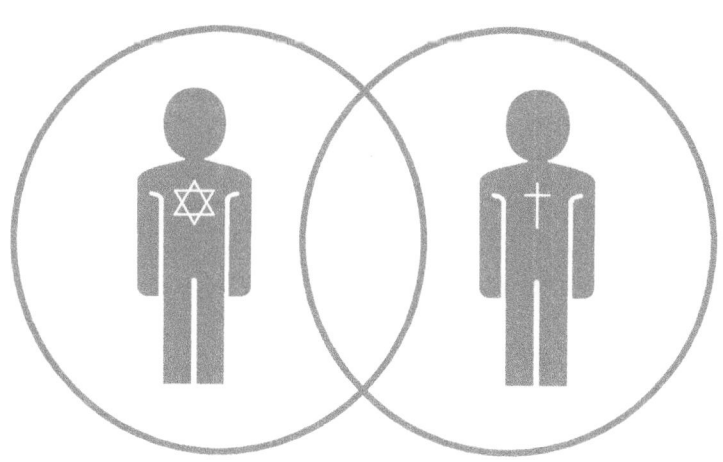

The Insiders of Special Revelation

13

Special Revelation:
Jewish Insiders *before* the Cross

What does the gospel say about the salvation of "Old Testament saints"? That is, what is the relationship between the faithful Jews who died before the Christ event and the faithfulness of Jesus Christ, and is there a continuing connection between God's covenant with Israel and the new covenant in Christ? To answer these questions, we have to understand the radical difference between Old Testament forgiveness (paresis) and New Testament forgiveness (aphesis).

THE FIRST COVENANT

What does the gospel have to say about the faithful Jews who lived and died before the cross? Christians sometimes refer to these people as "Old Testament saints." Having dealt with the *why* and *how* of divine forgiveness in the previous chapter, we now turn to a discussion of special revelation for these Old Testament saints and their relationship to the subsequent redemption that is in Jesus Christ.

Paul said the Law of Moses and the Old Testament prophets were witnesses *to* the righteousness of God rather than manifestations *of* that righteousness. He went on to say that separate and apart from the Law,

God's righteousness had been uniquely manifested in the space/time reality of the Christ event, and that sin can be forgiven or "justified" *only* through the faith *of* Jesus Christ (Rom 3:21–22 KJV). So where does that leave the Old Testament saints who died before the Christ event?

RETROACTIVE FORGIVENESS AND THE NEW COVENANT

Paul was referring to Christ in Rom 3:25, when he said, ". . . whom God displayed publicly as a propitiation in His blood through faith. This [redemption] was to demonstrate His [God's] righteousness, because in the forbearance of God He passed over *the sins previously committed*," that is, the sins committed before the cross.

In verse twenty-five, the apostle made a sweeping declaration that divine forgiveness has a special connotation for Old Testament saints. More specifically, he said there had been a merciful delay or "forbearance" *(anoche)* of divine judgment, and God had temporarily "passed over" *(paresis)* their sinful imperfections *until* the Christ event—where actual atonement was made for the sin of the whole world.

Without a doubt, Paul was saying that the Son's atonement and the Father's forgiveness were *retroactive* for these Old Testament saints! In order to fully appreciate the retroactive nature of God's grace, we need a clear understanding of divine forbearance *(anoche)* as well as the idea that God temporarily passed over *(paresis)* the sin of Old Testament saints:

Anoche is a compound word made up of *ana* (up) and *echo* (to hold or bear), so forbearance means "to hold up or hold back" like a dam holds back a river.

Paresis is also a compound word made up of *para* (by or beside) and *hiemi* (to send), and it means, "to send by or pass over."

"Forbearance" *(anoche)* can be further explained in relationship to the legal "consideration" that is required in order to have a binding contract. Most contracts use the phrase "$10.00 and other good and valuable considerations" as a recital of the "consideration" that turns a simple promise into a promise that is legally binding. Under the law, "consideration" can have either a positive or a negative connotation in an agreement. The giving of a promise or the payment of a deposit has a *positive* connotation because it means something has been given to bind the deal.

Forbearance, on the other hand, has a *negative* connotation because it means something is held back—like a person not doing something he had a right to do.

God's covenant with Israel contained both forms of consideration: God's promises were *"given"* to the fathers, and his forbearance *"held back"* judgment until the atonement of Christ could be accomplished (Rom 3:25). The use of "forbearance" in verse twenty-five means the execution of divine judgment against Old Testament saints was temporarily suspended.

Sin is always a serious matter; therefore, the sin of the "Old Testament saints" could not be ignored or written off. "Passed over" *(paresis)* must be understood in relationship to the fact that God hates sin. However, Paul said God "held back" his perfect judgment and temporarily "passed over" the sins "previously committed" by faithful Jews until *all* sin could be absolved on the cross. In those days God's perfect judgment temporarily "passed over" the sins of faithful Jews much like the death angel temporarily "passed over" the first born of the Israelites at the time of Israel's Exodus from Egypt, an event that Jewish people still celebrate as "Passover." One might say that Rom 3:25 is Judaism's ultimate "Passover"!

It should be noted, however, that the language of "forbearance" and "passed over" in Rom 3:25 does not apply to Jews guilty of unbelief *(apistia)*. Indeed, the apostle Paul indicated in chapter 11 of Romans that rebellious Jews had been eliminated from God's spiritual "olive tree." First covenant Jews faced radically different destinies. The sins of faithful Jews were temporarily passed over until sin's debt could be paid on the cross. But unfaithful Jews faced God's immediate judgment. Notwithstanding their covenant status as natural branches, "the rest were hardened," that is, "broken off" and separated from the holy root.

ATONEMENT AS EITHER PARESIS OR APHESIS

Any discussion of *"paresis"* as temporarily "passing by" Old Testament sin requires an expanded explanation regarding the difference between the Greek terms *paresis* (pass by) and *aphesis* (send away). The uniqueness of *paresis* is evident in its description as a "hapax," that is, something said only once. *Paresis* is a Greek word that is used in this one place in the New Testament in order to acknowledge that the guilt of Old Testament saints was temporarily held in abeyance until the eternal *aphesis* of Christ's atonement could sweep back in time and perfect their forgiveness.

The King James translation of the Bible (1611) complicated the situation by using the English word "remission" to translate both *paresis* and *aphesis*. There is a world of difference, however, between "remission" *(paresis)* in Rom 3:25 KJV and "remission" *(aphesis)* in Luke 24:47 KJV and Heb 9:22 KJV and other such passages. Both of these Greek terms contain the root word *hiemi*, which means, "to send." However, different prefixes can produce radically different meanings.

The Greek dramatizes the nuance between the two terms: *paresis* means God "sent by or passed by sin," while *aphesis* means God "sent the sin away." There is motion in both terms, but the meaning depends on the nature of the motion. With *paresis*, the sin problem is temporarily abated, and the spirit of God passes by, (like the death angel in Egypt). With *aphesis*, sin itself, is permanently sent away. As the Psalmist said, "He has not dealt with us according to our sins, Nor rewarded us according to our iniquities . . . As far as the east is from the west, So far has He removed our transgressions from us" (Ps 103:10, 12).

Israel's sacrificial system was critically important, but it did not wash away a single sin (Heb 10:4). Rather, it was *symbolic* and *temporary*. Old Testament sacrifices were symbolic because they meant that God had "passed by" *(paresis)* sin instead of eliminating the sin problem. They were temporary because God "held back" *(anoche)* his judgment of faithful Jews *until* the "fullness of time" (Gal 4:4) when the atonement of Christ would provide justification and open the door to eternal forgiveness *(aphesis)*.

DOUBLE EXPOSURE

A striking contrast regarding God's double treatment of sin occurs in Leviticus where Aaron the priest was directed to choose "two male goats for a sin offering" and to cast lots in order to designate "one lot for the Lord and the other lot for the scapegoat" (Lev 16: 5, 8).

The first goat was to be *killed* as a symbolic "sin offering" for the guilt of the people. Its blood was to be sprinkled "on the mercy seat and in front of the mercy seat *to make atonement* . . . because of the impurities

Special Revelation: Jewish Insiders before the Cross

of the sons of Israel, and because of their transgressions, and in regard to all their sins" (Lev 16: 9, 15, 16).

The second "scapegoat" was to be "presented *alive* before the Lord, *to make atonement upon it*, to send it into the wilderness ... Then Aaron shall lay both of his hands on the head of the live goat, and confess over it all the iniquities of the sons of Israel, and all their transgressions in regard to all their sins; and he shall lay them on the head of the goat and send it away into the wilderness by the hand of a man who stands in readiness. And the goat shall bear *on itself* all their iniquities to a solitary land; and he shall release the goat in the wilderness" (Lev 16: 10, 21–22).

Like overlapping images in a double-exposure photograph, the sacrificial goat and the scapegoat reveal that atonement is a double-exposure of death *and* life. Over a thousand years after Moses, the double-exposure actually came to pass in the death *and* life of Jesus Christ. His death was the way of sacrifice, and his resurrection was "the way, and the truth, and the life" (John 14:6). Crucifixion was the time and place of atonement, and resurrection was the proof that atonement had been made.

The writer of Hebrews confirms that special revelation has a two-fold application that carries over from the Old Testament to the New Testament. That is, "God, after He spoke long ago to the fathers in the prophets in many portions and in many ways, in these last days has spoken to us in His Son, whom He appointed heir of all things ... When He had made *purification* of sins, He sat down at the right hand of the Majesty on high" (Heb 1:1–3).

The English translation describes the work of atonement as "purification" *(katharismos)*, but the word picture is much less sanitized. Indeed, the Greek root gives us the English word "catharsis" with its multiple dictionary meanings. In medicine, it means "purgation or evacuation of the bowels"; in psychiatry, it means to "discharge pent-up emotions"; and in the arts it can refer to "purging the emotions of an audience." In other words, when Christ "made purification," he conquered sin and death and opened the door to God's forgiveness.

God-the-Father as perfect justice temporarily withheld judgment until God-the-Son as perfect love made atonement for sin. If Jesus is truly the "the light of the world," as the Bible says, then his "light" simultaneously radiates in all directions. His atonement and the Father's forgiveness flow back in time to purge the "sins previously committed" by Old

Testament saints (Rom 3:25), but it also flows forward in time as we shall see in the next chapter.

14

Special Revelation: Christian Insiders *after* the Cross

Everything changed when Christ said, "It is finished!" After the cross, the Old Testament need for forbearance and temporary forgiveness vanished, and all human beings are faced with immediate accountability. People now have to deal with either the consequences of accountability or the benefits of atonement.

THE NEW COVENANT

God has always had a zero tolerance for sin, but with special revelation as manifested in the Christ event, human history took a sharp turn. After Christ's atonement, the stopgap effect of Old Testament forbearance was no longer needed, and the temporary passing-by of *paresis* gave way either to immediate judgment or to the eternal forgiveness of *aphesis*. What was the nature of the change?

Aphesis is derived from the Greek verb *aphiemi*—a compound word made up of *apo* ("away from") and *hiemi* (to send). When compounded, it means "sending away" or "getting rid of completely" as in eternal forgiveness and remission of sin. With *aphesis* the forgiveness spotlight falls on the one who needs to be forgiven.

Whereas *paresis* indicates that God had temporarily "passed over" sin, *aphesis* means that the sin, itself, is permanently "sent away." Atonement was complete because the price for human disobedience had been paid. The once-for-all-time price Christ paid on the cross *satisfied* the requirements of perfect justice and *justified* sinful people (past, present, and future) *just as if* their sinful imperfection had never been an issue.

After the cross, *aphesis* could be used to explain divine forgiveness because the penalty for sin had been paid in full, and the temporary effect of "passing by" or "overlooking" sin was unnecessary. The theological transition from *paresis* to *aphesis* is reminiscent of shifts in technology where the horse and buggy gave way to motor vehicles, and eight-track tapes gave way to compact discs.

Furthermore, it is hard to ignore the timing of the transition from *paresis* to *aphesis*. The Jewish sacrificial system had been in place for over a thousand years dating back to Moses and the exodus from Egypt. Then, barely thirty-five years after Christ's atonement on the cross, the Roman general Titus destroyed the temple and ended Israel's symbolic sacrificial system. Thereafter, the idea of God's forbearance and the retroactive theology of *paresis* would be an anachronism, and the theology of *aphesis* could be used to explain the immediate effect of eternal forgiveness.

In trying to think of something that might help illustrate the difference between *paresis* and *aphesis,* I was reminded of an act of disobedience from my own childhood. My mother had purchased a pair of corduroy overalls for me to wear to school, and I hated them with a passion. The straps looped over the shoulders and snapped at the chest, and the pants hung loose instead of being belted at the waist like the blue jeans that "everybody else" wore. Thinking I wouldn't have to wear the baggy overalls if they got lost, I got rid of them. Instead of putting them in the laundry, I "hid" them in the top of the closet and told my mother I didn't know where they were. For whatever reason, my mother "passed by" the dirty overalls for a few days much like God passed by *(paresis)* the sinful imperfection of repentant Jews prior to the cross. However, her height eventually "revealed" the overalls in the top of the closet, and she confronted me with my misdeed. Needless to say, she dealt with my deception, but the point is that she then "got rid of" the hated overalls much like Christ got rid of *(aphesis)* our sin on the cross.

Special Revelation: Christian Insiders after *the Cross*

CHRIST'S ATONEMENT

It is critically important to remember that Christ's atonement was and is God's only remedy for sin, and that it occurred at one particular point in time and space. Contemporary science equates the two as "space-time." At that one particular point, sin was completely disposed of or "sent away." However, for Christ's atonement to be effective anytime and anywhere, it would have to have spiritual implications not only for the *present* but also for the *past* and the *future*.

As discussed in the previous chapter, total forgiveness of sin was not available under Israel's original sacrificial system. After the cross, however, the sin that had been temporarily "passed by" in the Old Testament was permanently "sent away." In other words, Christ's atonement operated *retrospectively* for the "saints" who lived before the cross (Rom 3:25), and it continues to operate *prospectively* for all the "saints" after the cross.

The question, of course, is how can an atonement that occurs in one place at one time in history (space-time) be understood to have an impact on both the past and the future?

LINEAR VERSUS NONLINEAR PERSPECTIVE

The thought of integrating *past, present,* and *future* brings to my mind the difference between linear and nonlinear phenomena:

On one hand, the human perspective of time is *linear*. Each interval of time has a beginning and an end. For the physical universe, including plants, animals, and human beings, creation is the "Mother" happening. It is the Alpha event that stretches out through time towards an Omega event that would end human existence, as we know it. In secular terms, the end could result from nuclear winter, climate change, or some other catastrophe. Theologically, "end-times" would be a matter of divine intervention. At any rate, we know that human events twist and turn through time like the Mississippi River meanders through the American heartland. The river always rolls on toward the Gulf of Mexico just as human experience rolls on through time. Regardless of scientific speculation and all the science fiction stories, humanity understands that time runs in one direction. We cannot go backwards in time any more than we can "un-ring" a bell!

Christianity and the Outsider

On the other hand, God's perspective of time is *nonlinear*. He is the infinite creator of all finite phenomena, including matter, time, and space. When one tries to imagine time and space from God's point of view, he has to think in nonlinear terms. Peter said, "... with the Lord one day is as a thousand years, and a thousand years as one day" (2 Pet 3:8). Paul alluded to God's mysterious "time machine" when he said, "But when the fullness of the time [*chronos* as in chronology] came, God sent forth His Son, born of a woman, born under the Law in order that He might redeem those who were under the Law..." (Gal 4:4–5).

Augustine of Hippo (354–430) was an influential philosopher and an early church father who taught that God represented a unique perspective regarding time, a point of view that I would describe as nonlinear. That is, human beings understand time as past, present, and future, but God is "the divine 'now'" who is omnipresent or the eternal present.[1] As the creator of matter, time, and space; God is not limited by matter, time, and space.

The Danish philosopher/theologian Soren Kierkegaard (1813–1855) visualized the nonlinear perspective of time and space long before Einstein's $E=mc^2$ revolutionized our understanding of time and space. In an 1835 journal entry, Kierkegaard said the ultimate reference point would be found by the "... solitary inquirer [whose] life will flow on peacefully and quietly, and he will neither drain the intoxicating cup of pride nor the bitter chalice of despair. He has found what the great philosopher ... desired, but did not find: that Archimedean point from which he could lift [or conceptualize] the whole world, the point which for that very reason must lie ... *outside* the limitations *of time and space*."[2] (Emphasis added)

Whereas God is outside or beyond matter, time and space, human beings are part of God's created matter, and we exist in the time and space that he created. Like fish living in a lake, we live in a space-time "lake." Contemplating earthly existence without time and space would be like imagining a fish without water. In Gal 4:4, Paul used the "passing of time" from one event to another to explain that when the "time" was right, God intervened in human time and space in the person of Jesus Christ. Needless to say, God's intervention in human history was an unparalleled event.

---

1. Jordan, "Augustine," 53.
2. Kierkegaard, "The Journals," 4.

Special Revelation: Christian Insiders after the Cross

God-as-Father provided the ultimate revelation when he "sent forth" (ex*apostello*) God-as-Son to interface with humankind. *Ex* is a prefix that denotes "origin" or the "point from which an action proceeds," and *apostello* means "to set apart" or "to send forth a person on a mission." As an "apostle," Paul himself was an *apostolos* who was "sent out" to spread the good news of God's grace. In other words, God-as-Father represents a point of origin that is *outside* time and space, and God-as-Son came *into* time and space to demonstrate God's righteousness and grace—and to make forgiveness available to sinful humanity. It is from God's nonlinear perspective that we must understand God's tripartite intervention as Creator, Lawgiver, and Redeemer:

> Redemption
> God's creation of the universe is confirmed
> When new life comes into the world.
> Accountability for sin is confirmed every time
> A person breaks the law, and
> Victory over sin is confirmed every time
> A person receives forgiveness for sin.

Five hundred years before the birth of Christ, the Greek tradition identified the *logos* with the *impersonal* order of the universe as manifested in knowledge, reason, and the "word." The Hebrew tradition, on the other hand, tells the story of a *personal* God who creates, speaks, and gets involved with his creation. From a Christian perspective, the cosmic nature of God's involvement with his creation reached its apex in the prologue of the fourth gospel where the eternal *logos* of divine reason is identified with the Emmanuel (God with us) who intervened in human history—"In the beginning was the Word (*logos*) and the Word was with God and the Word was God . . . And the Word became flesh and dwelt among us and we beheld his glory, glory as of the only begotten from the Father, full of grace and truth" (John 1:1, 14).

Whereas, Philo Judaeus (20 BCE-50 CE), a Jewish scholar who lived in Alexandria during Jesus' earthly ministry, tried to synthesize Hebrew and Greek thought by identifying the *logos* as a non-personal intermediary between divine perfection and human imperfection, John's prologue proclaims a model of understanding where the *logos* is revealed as the personal "He" who blends the past, present and future into a new reality, that is, "the kingdom of God." John identified Jesus of Nazareth as the messianic *logos* who was "in the beginning," who was "with God," and who "was God," and who "became flesh and dwelled among us" (John 1:1, 14).

One of the great ironies of history occurred during the trial that led up to Jesus' crucifixion. Unaware of the approaching atonement for sin, Caiaphas the high priest got it right when he said:

> You know nothing at all, nor do you take into account that it is expedient for you that one man should die for the people, and that the whole nation should not perish. Now this he did not say on his own initiative; but being high priest that year, he prophesied that Jesus was going to die for the nation; and not the nation only, but that He might also gather together into one the children of God who are scattered abroad (John 11:49-52).

As mentioned earlier, everything changed when God's ultimate revelation said, "It is finished." Yet there is a sense in which everything remains the same because sin remains the same. It doesn't matter whether sin occurs before or after the cross because the nonlinear effect of Christ's atonement on the cross provides both retrospective and prospective victory over sin.

Admittedly, the biblical covenants have given Jews and Christians a unique perspective, but that perspective also creates an extraordinary responsibility. As Luke 12:48 says, "And from everyone who has been given much shall much be required . . . " There are blessings and responsibilities for those living within God's special covenants. But, what are the consequences for having been left outside those historical covenants?

Part V
General Revelation: Life Without a Covenant

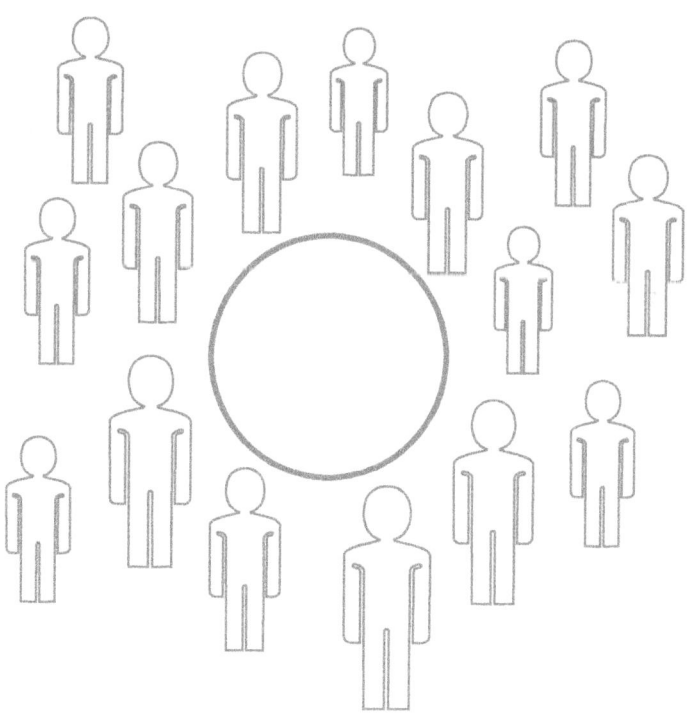

The Outsiders of General Revelation

15

General Revelation: Non-Jewish Outsiders *before* the Cross

The idea of general revelation suggests that God might have made his forgiveness available to "third party beneficiaries" even though they were strangers to the biblical covenants. For example, could some non-Jews in the Old Testament have been third party beneficiaries of God's grace even though they were excluded from God's covenant with Israel?

NON-JEWS BEFORE THE CROSS

As mentioned earlier, Rom 3:25 speaks of the forbearance *(anoche)* of God's judgment towards "Old Testament saints" and indicates that the atonement of Christ had a retroactive effect for these faithful Jews.

Could this divine forbearance toward "Old Testament saints" have also been available to people whom I will call "non-Jewish saints" for lack of a better term? And could Christ's atonement have had a retroactive impact on these non-Jewish "saints," just as it had a retroactive impact on the Jewish "saints"?

The Bible seems to suggest that God "held back" his judgment and temporarily "passed by" the sins of some non-Jews, just as he "held back" his judgment and temporarily "passed by" the sins of certain Jews.

The apostle Paul laid the groundwork for our discussion when he said, "For when Gentiles who do not have the Law do instinctively the things of the Law, these not having the Law, are a *law* to themselves, in that they show the work of the Law written in their hearts, their conscience bearing *witness*, and their thoughts alternately accusing or else defending them, on the day when according to my gospel, *God will judge the secrets* of men *through Christ Jesus*" (Rom 2:14–16).

Regarding these outsiders, I would argue that God's general revelation not only revealed "enough" *law* in each person's heart to produce accountability but also "enough" *witness* in each conscience to allow God to ultimately judge each person according to *the redemptive work of Jesus Christ* (Rom 2:14–16).

In Acts, Luke indicates that on at least two occasions during Paul's missionary ministry, he considered the retroactive impact of the Christ event on non-covenant (non-Jewish) people groups.

IN ACTS 14—GOD "PERMITTED"

In Acts 14 Barnabas and Paul were preaching the gospel in the non-Jewish city of Lystra. When they healed a Gentile who had been lame from birth, they received an overwhelming response from the people of Lystra. In Acts 14:11, the people said, "The gods have become like men and have come down to us." They thought Barnabas was Zeus, and the priest of Zeus wanted to offer a sacrifice and lead the people in worshiping the missionaries—But Barnabas and Paul said, "We are also men of the same nature as you." The apostle Paul then told the people about the "living God" and explained that "in the generations gone by He *permitted (eao)* all the nations *to go their own ways*; and yet He *did not leave Himself without witness, (amarturos)* in that He did good and gave you rains from heaven and fruitful seasons, satisfying your hearts with food and gladness" (Acts 14:11–15, 16–17).

"Permitted" is a translation of the Greek word *eao*, which means, "to let be, leave alone, suffer, or permit." So, regarding these outsiders in Lystra, the apostle said God "let them be" or "left them alone." Biblically speaking, during those "generations gone by," God's ultimate plan of redemption was unfolding in a special covenant with Israel. Clearly, during that period of time, the Gentiles were outside that covenant. However,

General Revelation: Non-Jewish Outsiders before the Cross

Luke's account quotes the apostle Paul as saying that "in generations gone by . . . [God] did not leave Himself without witness" *(amarturos)* to the Lycaonians (Acts 14:17). Apparently, God had some kind of ongoing witness to these outsiders—even before the cross.

Who was this "witness" who is mentioned indirectly in Acts 14:17? Note that in Greek, as in English, the letter "*a*" is added as a prefix to create the negative form as in "moral and *amoral*." Without the prefix, *marturos* is the word for a witness who testifies in court and is similar to the word Paul used in my earlier reference to Rom 2:15 where he said that even though the Gentiles were outsiders, their "consciences" *(suneidesis)* were "bearing witness" *(summartureo)* to the Law that was "written in their hearts." These two words have profound implications:

Suneidesis combines *sun* (with or together) and *eido* (to know intuitively) to mean something more profound than mere psychology. The apostle is speaking of an innate faculty within each human spirit that is confronted by the righteousness of God. As human beings, we must deal with the ultimate reality that we are not only created in the image of God, but we are also accountable to God.

Summartureo combines *sun* (with or together) and *martureo* (to be a witness or to testify) to create the idea of joint witnesses. In other words, it means, "to testify jointly" as when one witness corroborates the testimony of another witness.

The Greek text seems to indicate that God's general revelation had come to these non-Jews even though they were not privy to the special revelation that is reflected in Israel's sacrificial system. Certainly there was enough revelation to establish their accountability before God. Paul had already stated that the Spirit provides *personal* corroboration to all individuals "because that which is known about God is evident *within* them; for God made it evident to them. For since the creation of the world His invisible attributes, His eternal power and divine nature, have been clearly seen, being understood through what has been made, so that they are without excuse" (Rom 1:19–20).

We know that Paul was referring to both insiders and outsiders because in the next chapter, he said, ". . . there is no partiality with God. For all who have sinned without the Law will also perish without the Law; and all who have sinned under the Law will be judged by the Law; for not the hearers of the Law are just before God, but the doers of the Law will be justified" (Rom 2:11–13).

Christianity and the Outsider

Paul goes on to speak specifically of God's relationship with non-Jewish outsiders. On one hand, the Spirit of God has written the law *"in the hearts"* of these Gentiles and has held them accountable for their sin. On the other hand, the human spirit or "conscience" must respond to that accountability. In other words, these outsiders are personally accountable for their sin, and the human spirit must respond to the inward witness of the Holy Spirit—"their thoughts alternately accusing or else defending them." And what is the payoff for the accountability of these "generations gone by" that had never heard the gospel? Paul said God would judge them like everyone else. That is, "God will *judge* the secrets of men *through* Jesus Christ" (Rom 2:15–16).

The idea of universal accountability for insiders and outsiders takes us back to Rom 1:18 where the apostle Paul said, "For the wrath of God is revealed from heaven against *all* ungodliness," that is, against Jews and non-Jews. So how did these Old Testament outsiders know they were accountable to God? The Spirit of God bore witness to each individual spirit regarding his or her spiritual culpability.

Furthermore, the apostle Paul confirmed the idea of a corroborating witness *(summartureo)* in other Scriptures. In Rom 8:16, he said "The Spirit Himself bears witness *(summartureo)* with our spirit that *we are children of God.*" And in Rom 9:1, Paul referred to his own spirit as "bearing me witness *(summartureo)* in the Holy Spirit" regarding the truthfulness of his work. If the Holy Spirit gives positive witness that insiders are "children of God," then it follows that the Spirit also give negative witness to outsiders regarding their inherent accountability for sin.

Clearly, the "witness" to "generations gone by" in Acts 14 was not part of the "special revelation" that is associated with the covenant God made with Abraham. Therefore, it must be characterized as part of God's "general revelation." In other words, general revelation in Acts 14 must be considered not only in the context of *creation* but also in relationship to the *law* and to the *Christ event*. God's general *law* would have been at work convicting people of sin because they are a "law to themselves, in that they show the work of the Law written in their hearts" (Rom 2:15). And the *witness* of the Spirit would have been at work determining the nature and extent of their accountability, because "God will judge the secrets of men through Jesus Christ" (Rom 2:16).

There is a radical distinction between the work of the law and the justification that results from the Christ event. On one hand, "By the works of the Law *no* flesh will be *justified* . . . for through the Law comes the knowledge of sin (Rom 3:20). On the other hand, "being *justified* (is) a gift by His grace through the redemption which is in Christ Jesus" (Rom 3:24).

Admittedly, the Lycaonians were accountable to God for their sin, but the apostle Paul made it clear that God would not judge these outsiders according to his ancient covenant with Israel. Instead, God judged these outsiders according to the law that was "written in their hearts" and according to the inward witness of the Spirit of God. Paul drove home the idea of "inward" accountability in verse sixteen, when he said God would not only "judge the *secrets*" of these outsiders, but would judge them "*through* Christ Jesus" (Rom 2:14–16).

Luke's gospel teaches that there are varying degrees of accountability, that is, ". . . the one who did not know it [the master's will] and committed deeds worthy of a flogging, will receive but few. And from everyone who has been given much shall much be required" (Luke 12:48). In view of Luke's statements regarding the degrees of accountability, it appears that a person's understanding of the will of God would definitely have some impact on the nature and extent of his or her accountability to God.

However, as mentioned earlier, the critical issue is not how much we know about God, but what God knows about us—and we know he knows everything about us! How much would the people of Lystra have to have known about God? They would have to have known *enough* to realize "the wrath of God . . . against all ungodliness" (Rom 1:18), *enough* to experience the repentance that is involved in "a broken and contrite heart (Ps 51:17), and *enough* for God's "forbearance" to hold back judgment (Rom 3:25) until the atonement of Jesus Christ could pay the price for sin. The ethical reference to doing "good" and the spiritual reference to having "gladness" of heart in Acts 14:17 suggest that Paul had something more in mind than the general revelation of creation.

Of course, the human spirit can be trained or "hardened" against the witness of the Spirit of God. The writer of Hebrews spoke of this problem in a warning that echoes all the way back to Moses—"Today if you hear His voice, do not harden your hearts" (Heb 3:13–16, Ps 95:7–8).

Some traditionalists will argue that judging the "secrets of men through Christ Jesus" in Romans 2:16 is just another reference to special revelation. However, I would contend that Paul had general revelation in

Christianity and the Outsider

mind rather than special revelation because verses fourteen, fifteen, and sixteen are clearly directed at outsiders rather than covenant insiders.

IN ACTS 17—GOD "OVERLOOKED"

A few years ago, I stood on Mars Hill and looked out over the City of Athens just as the apostle Paul did two thousand years ago. I thought about what must have been going through his mind as he prepared to speak to the local leaders and intellectuals. Paul was highly educated, so he would have known about the philosophy, literature, and other aspects of the "Golden Age" of Greece (500–400 BCE). He would also have understood the vanity that allowed the Greeks to denigrate "outsiders" by dividing the world into "Greeks and barbarians," just as Israel had divided the world into "Jews and Gentiles."

Paul began his sermon by complimenting the Greeks on their spirituality. He referred specifically to their altar "To An Unknown God" and said, "What therefore you worship in ignorance, this I proclaim to you." He then went on to introduce them to "The God who made the world and all things in it, since He is Lord of heaven and earth, does not dwell in temples made with hands . . . and He made from one, every nation of mankind to live on all the face of the earth . . . that they should seek God, if perhaps they might *grope for* Him *and find* Him, though *He is not far from each one of us . . .* " (Acts 17:22-27). Clearly, the apostle's initial approach was an appeal to the Athenians in the context of God's concern for *all* people.

The apostle then narrowed the parameters of the discussion and said, "Therefore having overlooked *(hypereido)* the times of ignorance, God is now declaring to men that *all everywhere* should repent, because He has fixed a day in which He will judge the world in righteousness through a Man whom He has appointed, having furnished proof to all men by raising Him from the dead" (Acts 17:30-31). I would suggest that Paul's double emphasis that "all" people, "everywhere" should repent would seem to apply to both insiders and outsiders.

The key to understanding this passage is to realize that *hypereido* is a Greek compound that joins *hyper* (over or beyond) and *eido* (to see) in order to explain that God had temporarily "overlooked" or was "looking

General Revelation: Non-Jewish Outsiders before the Cross

beyond" the ignorance of some Athenians even though they were strangers to his covenant with Israel.

The King James translation is especially interesting at this point because it says that in former times God "winked" *(hypereido)* at the ignorance of people who were outside God's special covenant with Israel. "Winked" does not mean that God was nonchalant about the sinfulness of these outsiders. Instead, God "overlooked" or "winked" at the *noncovenant ignorance* of some non-Jews (Acts 17:30) just as he "passed over" the *first covenant knowledge* of certain Jews (Rom 3:25)—until Christ paid the price for sin on the cross. The point is that the "repentance for forgiveness" that Jesus proclaimed in Luke 24:47 is not based upon what one knows, but whether one has repented of his or her anti-God self-righteousness. Apparently, God's temporary forbearance was applicable to both Jews and non-Jews, and it was to last until he would "judge the world" through Jesus Christ (Acts 17:30–31).

The situation in Old Testament times was that God *passed over* (Rom 3:25), *permitted* (Acts 14:16), and *overlooked* (Acts 17:30) the sinful imperfection of some Jews *and* some non-Jews until a future time when God would "judge the world in righteousness through a Man." Jesus was the man who would be raised up on a cross *to pay* the penalty for sin and then raised from the dead *to prove* the authenticity of the price that had been paid (Acts 17:31).

Clearly these Acts 14 and 17 Scriptures put Old Testament Gentiles outside God's special covenant with Israel, and therefore, beyond the scope of special revelation. If God "held back" his judgment against some of these "outsiders," it would have to have been part of God's general revelation, that is, part of the "unsearchable" and "unfathomable" providence of God that the apostle mentioned in Rom 11:33.

Regarding covenant insiders, ". . . God sent forth His Son, born of a woman, born under the [Mosaic] Law, in order that He might redeem those who were under the Law, that we might receive the adoption as sons" (Gal 4:4–5).

But regarding covenant outsiders, ". . . these, not having a Law, are a law to themselves, in that they show the work of the Law written in their hearts, [and] God will judge the secrets of men through Christ Jesus" (Rom 2:14–15). God-as-Son was "raised up" from a manger, "raised up" on a cross, and "raised up" from the grave as proof that he was the Emmanuel of "God with us."

Paul seems to have contemplated the destiny of both the Jews and the non-Jews who had lived before the Christ event. Regarding the Jewish insiders, he said God temporarily "held back" his judgment and "passed over" the sins of faithful first covenant Jews (Rom 3:25). As to the non-Jews, Paul said God had "permitted" or "overlooked" or "winked" at the sins of some of these outsiders.

It would appear, therefore, that God "held back" his judgment and temporarily "passed by" the sinful imperfections of repentant Jews (special revelation) and repentant non-Jews (general revelation) until Christ's atonement could provide justification for their sinful imperfection.

But where is the rationale that could put non-Jews in the same category with Jews? Simply put, Old Testament Gentiles were convicted by "the work of the [general] law written in their hearts" (Rom 2:15). In other words, they knew intuitively that God would hold them accountable for their sin. The real question is whether they repented of their anti-God state of mind. As the apostle Paul said, God would eventually judge those "secrets . . . through Christ Jesus" (Rom 2:16).

Indeed, Old Testament Jews and Gentiles were under equal condemnation for their anti-God state of mind. Like Job, some of these nameless people humbled themselves before the God of the universe (Job 42:6), and some did not. The humbling of Naaman (2 Kings 5) and Nebuchadnezzar (Daniel 4) before "the Most High . . . King of heaven" are examples of Old Testament outsiders who humbled themselves before God without actually becoming part of God's special covenant with Israel. They repented, and God temporarily held back his judgment until a time when the retroactive *atonement* of God-as-Son and the *forgiveness* of God-as-Father would do the rest. What is the difference between repentance and redemption?

1. *Personal repentance* is a condition precedent to God's plan of redemption, but it is not part of that plan. Repentance is the humbling of pride and self-righteousness. It is a matter of what the sinner cannot do rather than what he can do—That is, he cannot save himself. Repentance is passive and negative rather than active and positive. Like a drowning man realizing that he cannot save himself, repentance is the sinner surrendering to spiritual death.

2. *Redemption* is a two-sided gift that works like a pair of saddlebags: One side of redemption is the *atonement* of God-as-Son.

Atonement means that the Son has paid the price for sin. The sinner receives justification because the Son has taken the blame for the sinner's anti-God state of mind. In bookkeeping terms, Christ has paid a debt owed by the sinner, and his account is justified with a zero balance. The other side of redemption is the *forgiveness* of God-as-Father. Having been justified by the Son's atonement, the repentant sinner receives the Father's forgiveness—"Though your sins are as scarlet, They will be as white as snow; Though they are red like crimson, They will be like wool" (Isa 1:18).

Justification and forgiveness are not earned. Therefore, divine redemption does not depend upon what a person knows or does. Indeed, whether one is a Jewish insider, a Christian insider, or a non-covenant outsider, the only thing that matters is whether one has *repented* of his or her sin.

Even as far back as Job, possibly the oldest book in the Bible, people were trying to solve the mystery surrounding a person's relationship to God. But in the final analysis, the only thing Job could say was, "I have heard of Thee by the hearing of the ear; But now my eye sees Thee; Therefore, I retract, And I *repent* in dust and ashes" (Job 42:5–5).

Furthermore, it should be noted that Job had made an earlier affirmation of his *faith* when he said, "I know that my Redeemer lives, And at the last He will take His stand on the earth. Even after my skin is destroyed, Yet from my flesh I shall see God; Whom I myself shall behold, And whom my eyes shall see and not another" (Job 19:25–27.) Job made a profession of faith in Job 19, but apparently it was his repentance in Job 42 that put him in right relationship with the God of the universe.

Chapter 15 has been a discussion of general revelation in connection with Christ's atonement for the sinful imperfection of the non-covenant "outsiders" who lived before the cross. As with Israel's special revelation, general revelation means the *repentance* of an outsider would have been followed by the divine forbearance that delayed judgment.

The outsider's redemption would then have been completed with the retroactive effect of the Son's atonement and the Father's forgiveness. In other words, Christ's atonement would provide retroactive justification for sin "previously committed" (Rom 3:25), "permitted" (Acts 14:16), or "overlooked" (Acts 17:30). Jesus confirmed the redemptive sequence when he closed Luke's gospel with the statement that "repentance for forgiveness of sins" should be proclaimed to the whole world (Luke 24:47).

In the next three chapters, we must turn our attention to the eternal destiny of "outsiders" after the cross, especially the chapter 18 discussion of whether non-covenant outsiders are even capable of repentance in connection with their anti-God state-of-mind.

16

General Revelation: Non-Christian Outsiders *after* the Cross

If non-Christian outsiders have general accountability for sin, even though they are not privy to the "new covenant," is it possible that God may have provided a general remedy from sin that is beyond the limited understanding of Christian insiders?

NON-CHRISTIAN OUTSIDERS (JEWISH AND NON-JEWISH): AFTER THE CROSS

The dilemma is that both covenant insiders and outsiders are understood to have general accountability *for sin*, but the remedy *from sin* is traditionally limited to Christian insiders who were or are privy to the new covenant.

From time to time the Scripture cautions covenant insiders against trying to limit God's power. For example, Israel complained to Moses during the Exodus, "And the Lord said to Moses, 'Is the Lord's power limited? Now you shall see whether My word will come true for you or not'" (Num 11:23). And when the prophet Isaiah was holding the Israelites accountable for their approaching exile, the Lord said, "Is My hand so short that it cannot ransom? Or have I no power to deliver? Behold, I dry up the sea with My rebuke, I make the rivers a wilderness" (Isa 50:2).

Later the prophet Isaiah told the Israelites that God's objectives could be accomplished even through pagan outsiders. Cautioning the Israelites about their unfaithfulness, the prophet said, "Who has believed our message? And to whom has the arm of the Lord been revealed" (Isa 53:1). And later, "I permitted Myself to be sought by those who did not ask for me. I said, 'Here am I, here am I,' to a nation which did not call on My name" (Isa 65:1)? Some might wonder if the power of God is too weak or the arm of the Lord too short to reach outsiders who are not privy to the new covenant, but the Bible says, ". . . with God all things are possible" (Matt 19:26).

If the long arm of the Father's judgment could reach out beyond Israel's covenant in order to carry out God's will, then perhaps the Son's arm of atonement is long enough to reach out beyond the new covenant.

Furthermore, if the *retroactive* effect of the atonement of Christ could reach back in time to first covenant Jews and non-covenant Gentiles, then it goes without saying that the *prospective* effect of Christ's atonement is able to reach forward in time. Indeed, the central premise of the Christian church is that Christ's atonement two thousand years ago operates prospectively to provide justification and forgiveness for Christian insiders under the new covenant.

The question is whether the future impact of Christ's atonement is limited to insiders who are *privy* to the new covenant, or is it possible that the providence of God has made justification available to some who are *not privy* to that covenant. And if so, who and how?

If the Father's arm of forgiveness is long enough to reach non-Jews *before* the cross even though they were not privy to God's covenant with Israel, can it be argued that his arm of forgiveness is long enough to reach non-Christians *after* the cross even though they are not privy to the new covenant?

The notion of general revelation after the cross is the climax of this study. It is both complex and controversial because it raises the possibility of New Testament forgiveness *(aphesis)* for some who are strangers to the new covenant. The seriousness of the issue justifies a recap of the argument, before we try to expand the idea of general revelation in this chapter:

General Revelation: Non-Christian Outsiders after the Cross

Part I introduced the insider/outsider problem as the "scandal of exclusivity" and focused on the theological dilemma that faces the outsiders who have been excluded from the biblical covenants.

Part II explained creation, law, and the Christ event as *general revelation* in the sense that all three have universal impact on all people. However, the law and the Christ event also have *special revelation* implications in connection with God's initial covenant with Israel and with the new covenant in Christ.

Part III used the constant speed of light in $E=mc^2$ as a metaphor for the constant Christ of Heb 13:8 who is the same "yesterday, today, and forever," and argued that the science of special and general relativity is a model for the theology of special and general revelation.

Part IV discussed *special revelation* in connection with God's covenant with Israel (the Jewish insiders) and the new covenant in Christ (the Christian insiders): Chapter 13 reviewed the retroactive nature of God's special remedy for "Old Testament saints," and chapter 14 examined the prospective nature of God's special remedy for "New Testament saints." It must be remembered, however, that merely being privy to a biblical covenant is not salvific.

Part V is a discussion of *general revelation* in connection with the lives of covenant outsiders both before and after the cross:

Chapter 15 used the language of Rom 2:14–16, Acts 14:16–17, and Acts 17:30–31 to argue the possibility of a general remedy for Gentiles before the cross who were not privy to God's covenant with Israel. Furthermore, the same rationale applies to Gentiles after the cross who were not or are not privy to the new covenant.

Chapter 16 now seeks to expand the discussion of general revelation in order to show that divine providence may also have provided a general remedy for some Jews after the cross—even though they were not or are not privy to the new covenant. The discussion begins with the unique relationship between the Old Testament and the New Testament. That is, what is the connection between God's covenant with Israel and the new covenant in Christ, and what is the destiny of faithful Jews who do not acknowledge Jesus as Israel's Messiah?

ISRAEL'S RESPONSE TO THE CHRIST EVENT: ROMANS 9-11

In chapters 9 through 11 of Romans, the apostle Paul turns his attention to the relationship between God's covenant with Israel and the new covenant in Christ. The Old Testament and the New Testament not only recognize both covenants but also refer to the "new covenant" as God's ultimate initiative. In the Old Testament, the prophet Jeremiah said, "Behold, days are coming . . . when I will make a *new covenant* with the house of Israel and with the house of Judah . . . I will put My law within them, and on their heart I will write it; and I will be their God, and they shall be My people" (Jer 31:31,33).

New Testament writers not only refer to both covenants but go out of their way to connect the two covenants. For example, the writer of Hebrews said, "For if the blood of goats and bulls and the ashes of a heifer sprinkling those who have been defiled, sanctify for the cleansing of the flesh, how much more will the blood of Christ . . . cleanse your conscience from dead works to serve the living God? And for this reason He is the mediator of a *new covenant,* in order that since a death has taken place for the redemption of the transgressions that were committed under the *first covenant,* those who have been *called* may receive the promise of the eternal inheritance" (Heb 9:13-15).[1]

In Heb 9:15, the writer of Hebrews was appealing to first covenant Jews who were outsiders to the new covenant just as the apostle Paul had referred to Gentiles who were outsiders to God's covenant with Israel in Rom 2:15. Indeed, the writer of Hebrews used "conscience" *(suneidesis)* regarding these Jewish outsiders just as Paul did with the Gentile outsiders in Acts 14:16. As mentioned earlier, these writers used the term *suneidesis* to refer to the human spirit being confronted by the Spirit of God rather than the mere subjectivity of the human conscience as in psychology.

It's clear that the early church embraced both covenants. For example, Peter's ministry was initially focused on a church that was primarily Jewish, but it later expanded to include non-Jews. Indeed, Peter celebrated the expanded ministry when he described the people of the new covenant as ". . . a chosen race, a royal priesthood, a holy nation, a people for God's own possession, that you may proclaim the excellencies of Him who has called you out of darkness into his marvelous light" (1 Pet 2:9).

---

1. Regarding, a better covenant and better promises, see Heb 8:6-13 and 12:24.

General Revelation: Non-Christian Outsiders after the Cross

The apostle Paul's primary ministry was to open the new covenant to the Gentiles, but he also worried about the first covenant Jews who had rejected the new covenant. He embraced the new covenant, but he agonized over the fact that so many of his "kinsmen" denied that Jesus was the Messiah. In fact, the apostle began chapter 9 of Romans with a passionate expression of grief concerning the situation. He said, "I could wish that I myself were accursed, separated from Christ for the sake of my brethren, my kinsmen according to the flesh" (Rom 9:2).

Parenthetically, it should be noted that my discussion of these two covenants is not an endorsement of the two covenant doctrine that some people identify as "supersessionism" and others refer to as "replacement theology"—that is, that Israel was God's "chosen people," that Israel rejected Christ, and that God then turned to Christianity as the exclusive vehicle for the fulfillment of his promise of an "eternal inheritance." Also, it is not an endorsement of the equal opportunity idea that the Jews have the Law of Moses, the Christians have the law of Christ, and that they are mutually exclusive. The apostle Paul makes it clear that God is not finished with the Jews even though collective Israel has rejected Christ as the promised Messiah.

Toward the end of the chapter 11, Paul indicated that God has a continuing relationship with some Jews notwithstanding their response to Israel's Messiah. He said, "From the standpoint of the gospel they are *enemies* for your sake, but from the standpoint of God's choice they are *beloved* for the sake of the fathers" (Rom 11:28–29). In spite of Israel's collective rejection of the new covenant, there is a providential connection between God and Israel. Paul seems to have recognized that the first covenant and the new covenant have a side-by-side relationship even after the cross. I am suggesting, therefore, that contemporary Christians need to do some soul searching regarding the complex issues of Romans 9–11, and the first problem is identifying "Israel."

ISRAEL'S FIVE CATEGORIES

In order to avoid over-generalizations, we must distinguish between collective Judaism, traditional Jews as individuals, and Messianic Jews as individuals:

Christianity and the Outsider

First, one must acknowledge *collective Israel* as traditional Judaism. In spite of its various factions, Judaism shares a commonality in terms of land, language, history, and religion. Regardless of the struggles and persecutions of the past, Judaism seeks to remain faithful to its covenant with God, but Paul said, "That which [collective] Israel is seeking for, *it has not obtained* . . . " (Rom 11:7a). Paul had "great sorrow and unceasing grief" in his heart (Rom 9:2), because his kinsmen had collectively rejected the Messiah and his "new covenant."

Second, one must acknowledge Israel in terms of the *individual* lives of *traditional Jews*:

a) Regardless of collective Israel's failure to obtain that which it was seeking and in spite of the fact that some first covenant individuals were and are "enemies of the gospel" (Rom 11:28), "*those who were chosen obtain it*" (Rom 11:7b). (I will discuss the connection between the Old Testament remnant and this New Testament remnant in the next chapter.)

b) However, some first covenant insiders were like King Ahab before the cross and Jewish atheists, agnostics, etc. after the cross. That is, their anti-God state of mind showed they were unrepentant. Referring to these rebellious insiders, Paul said, ". . . *the rest were hardened*" (Rom 11:7c).

Third, and now outside traditional Judaism, one must acknowledge Israel in terms of the *individual* lives of *non-traditional Jews*. Sometimes referred to as "Messianic Jews," these individuals have responded to the "new covenant." Peter, Paul, and other early Jews embraced the new covenant, and over the years increasing numbers of non-traditional Jews have become part of the new covenant. As is the case with Gentiles, Messianic Jews are privy to the new covenant, therefore: The repentant sinner is justified by Christ's atonement, and, the unrepentant sinner with his anti-God state of mind is condemned. For example, a Jewish child can be privy to the new covenant by virtue of parents who are Messianic Jews, but his or her insider status does not guarantee salvation any more than insider status guarantees salvation in a Gentile home.

General Revelation: Non-Christian Outsiders after the Cross

THE BLESSINGS AND TRANSGRESSIONS OF ROM 9-11

Romans 9

Paul began chapter 9 of Romans with Israel's *collective blessings.* Israel enjoyed extraordinary blessings from God, notwithstanding her eventual rejection of the new covenant. Israel had the "adoption as sons and the glory and the covenants and the giving of the Law and the temple services and the promises" (Rom 9:4). And, of course, Jesus, himself, was a Jew (Rom 9:5).

However, after acknowledging Israel's special relationship with God, Paul asked a probing question—"who are Israelites? . . . For they are not all Israel who are descended from Israel; neither are they all children because they are Abraham's descendants . . . Through Isaac your descendants will be named. That is, it is not the children of the flesh who are children of God, but the children of the *promise* are regarded as descendants" (Rom 9:4, 6–8).

Luke was Paul's physician and traveling companion, and he shows John the Baptist totally dismissing Israel's legacy claim. John went so far as to say, "God is able from these *stones* to raise up children to Abraham" (Luke 3:8). Paul identified the "children of the promise" as the "descendants" who are to receive the "eternal inheritance," an inheritance that is to be made available to both Jews and non-Jews.

The relationship between the first covenant and the new covenant is complicated, but it is the key to understanding God's strategy for making the "riches of His glory" available not only to the "children of God" who are Jews but also to the "children of God" who are non-Jews. What does Paul say about the salvation or "eternal inheritance" that is available to both of these groups?

With the mystery of the man "who wills" versus the man "who resists" in full view (Rom 9:16 and 19), Paul described God's plan of redemption as having been prepared "beforehand"—that is, preordained or predestined. He said, "What if God . . . endured with much patience vessels of wrath prepared for destruction? And did so in order that He might make known the riches of His glory upon vessels of mercy which He prepared beforehand for glory, even us whom He also called, not from among *Jews* only, but also from among *Gentiles*" (Rom 9:22–24).

Christianity and the Outsider

Paul would later acknowledge that Israel's first covenant "calling" was and is "irrevocable" (Rom 11:28), but in Rom 9:24 he says new covenant Gentiles are "also called." Perhaps for the first time, Jews and non-Jews are jointly identified as beneficiaries of God's "eternal inheritance."

Romans 10

In chapter 10, Paul focused on Israel's *collective transgressions* as opposed to the collective blessings mentioned in chapter 9. He quoted Moses who said God would make the nation of Israel jealous, "By that which is not a nation, by a nation without understanding" (Rom 10:19). The apostle also quoted Isaiah who said, "But as for [collective] Israel He says, All day long I have stretched out my hands to a disobedient and obstinate people" (Rom 10:21).

Israel's blessings *and* transgressions were part of God's redemptive providence, and both were in play even before the Christ event. Israel's blessings were in view at the beginning of the first covenant when God said, "I will bless you . . . And so you shall be a blessing; And I will bless those who bless you . . . And in you all the families of the earth shall be blessed" (Gen 12:2-3).

Collectively, the apostle Paul created a sharp contrast between Israel's blessings and transgressions. On the negative side, he quoted Hosea as saying, "I will call those who were not my people, my people" (Rom 9:25). Moses even used a term that means "stiff-necked" when he referred to the collective "stubbornness" of Israel (Deut 31:27). On the positive side, Paul quoted Isaiah as saying, "Though the number of the sons of Israel be as the sand of the sea, it is the *remnant* that will be saved" (Rom 9:27). So who are the people who make up the remnant?

Individually, Old Testament Jews and non-Jews are like New Testament Jews and non-Jews in the sense that *all* have sinned, and *all* are accountable for their anti-God state of mind. However, *some* repent, and *some* do not. God's strategic plan of redemption was rolled out in the first covenant and then completed with the new covenant. Whether it is before or after the cross, the collective plan of salvation is carried out in the individual lives of both Jews and non-Jews. Before the cross, faithful individuals like Elijah found favor with God, and unfaithful individuals like Ahab rebelled against God—After the cross, faithful individuals like the apostle

Paul found favor with God, and unfaithful individuals like Judas Iscariot rebelled against God. Writing primarily to a new covenant audience, the apostle quoted a first covenant prophet when he said, "Whoever will call upon the name of the Lord will be saved" (Rom 10:13).

The writer of Hebrews put the old and the new covenants in proper perspective when he said, "But when Christ appeared as a high priest of the good things to come, He entered through the . . . tabernacle, not made with hands, that is to say, not of this creation" (Heb 9:11). After contrasting the blood of sacrificial animals with the blood of Christ, he went on to say, "And for this reason He [Christ] is the mediator of a *new covenant*, in order that since a death has taken place for the redemption of the transgressions that were committed under that first covenant,[2] those who have been called may receive the promise of the eternal inheritance" (Heb 9:15). Clearly, the promise of an "eternal inheritance" is the common denominator between both the first covenant and the new covenant.

Romans 11

In Romans 11, Paul acknowledged that *collective Israel* had rejected the new covenant, but he cushioned the indictment regarding *individual Jews*. The explanation is that Israel's collective "rejection" was part of a strategic plan that God had prepared beforehand in order to "reconcile" the world to himself (Rom 11:30 32).

Collectively, "first covenant" Israel may have rejected the "new covenant," but Paul said God had not rejected "His people" as individuals. Indeed, Paul viewed collective Israel's rejection of the new covenant as providential. He said, "God has *not* rejected His people . . . But by their [collective] transgression salvation has come to the Gentiles . . . Now if their [collective] transgression be riches for the world and their [collective] failure be riches for the Gentiles, how much more will their [individual] fulfillment be! . . . For if their [collective] rejection be the reconciliation of the world, what will their [individual] acceptance be but life from the dead" (Rom 11:1, 11–12, 15)?

Paul went on to say, "For just as you [non-Jews] once were [collectively] disobedient to God but now have been shown mercy because of

---

2. See Rom 3:25 and my discussion of the retroactive effect of Christ's atonement for sins "committed under that first covenant."

Christianity and the Outsider

their [collective] disobedience, so these [Jews] also now have been [collectively] disobedient, in order that because of the mercy shown to you they also may now be shown mercy. For God has shut up *all* in disobedience that He might show mercy to *all*" (Rom 11:30–32).

Israel's collective disobedience regarding the new covenant was an instrument of God's providence for reconciling the world to himself, just as the collective disobedience of the Gentile nations had been an instrument of God's providence in former times. Collective Israel, usually referred to as traditional Judaism, continues to cling to the first covenant. But does that mean that *individual* Jews are automatically excluded from the atonement that was made available through the cross?

Perhaps the *retroactive* effect of the atonement that formerly radiated *into the past* for first covenant Jews and non-covenant Gentiles now has a *prospective* effect that radiates *into the future* for first covenant Jews and non-covenant Gentiles.

We need to remember that "... there is no partiality with God" (Rom 2:11). The first few chapters in Romans confirm that first covenant insiders and outsiders as well as new covenant insiders and outsiders are equally and individually accountable to God. The good fortune of being privy to the first covenant, the new covenant, or both covenants does not guarantee that a person is right with God—Mere privity to either the first covenant or the new covenant does not guarantee the "eternal inheritance"!

We also need to be aware that the atonement of Christ cuts across time and space in order to deal with sin whenever and wherever it occurs. And it does not matter whether the sin was "passed by" *(paresis)* before the cross (Rom 3:24) or is "sent away" *(aphesis)* after the cross (Luke 24:47, Heb 9:22).

Generally speaking, Christians understand Christ's atonement in terms of *special revelation* and view it as available only to individuals who are privy to the new covenant. However, what if *general revelation* means that Christ's atonement is also available to some people who are strangers to the new covenant? As the apostle Paul said, that would, indeed, be "life from the dead" (Rom 11:15).

17

Paul's Olive Tree:
Insiders and Outsiders on the Same Tree?

Is it possible that Paul's "olive tree" in Romans 11 might contain branches representing Gentile Christians and Messianic Jews who are privy to the new covenant as well as the "chosen" Jews of Rom 11:7 who are privy only to the earlier covenant?

NATURAL OLIVE TREES VS. WILD OLIVE TREES

The study of general revelation becomes even more fascinating with the olive tree illustration that runs from Rom 11:16 through Rom 11:24. Most Christians understand Paul's illustration to be a continuation of the general indictment against Israel that began in Rom 9. However, a closer look at Paul's olive tree differentiates between collective Israel and individual Jews and suggests that the apostle was communicating a deeper meaning.

The illustration is built around an extended discussion regarding the nature of olive trees. Paul described two types of olive trees *(elaia)*. The good olive tree *(kallielaios)* is a tree that has been domesticated and cultivated for its fruit; the *kalli* prefix means the "good or better" olive tree. The wild olive tree *(agrielaios)* is a thrown-away tree that grows out in the field; its *agri* prefix means "field or country" *(agros)*, as seen in the word

Christianity and the Outsider

agriculture. In other words, the "better" tree is cultivated while the "wild" tree is ignored and unattended.

Growing up in Florida's citrus belt, I worked in the citrus industry and even owned an orange grove at one time, and I have firsthand experience with the dramatic contrast Paul described. Cultivated trees receive a lot of attention. The nursery stock is pampered, and then the trees are planted with great care. Thereafter, the trees are irrigated, fertilized, sprayed, plowed, pruned, etc. The economy of the whole region is dependent upon the citrus industry, so the cultivation of the trees and the harvesting of the fruit are important for the whole community.

I remember, however, that sometimes an orange tree would be located out in the woods or in the middle of a cow pasture because a bird had dropped a seed or there had been some other inadvertence. Needless to say, no one pays much attention to these "wild" trees. They are isolated and subjected to dry weather, freezing temperatures, and other natural hazards. Even a wild orange tree produces a few oranges, but the wild fruit is ignored because harvesting at random locations is not cost effective. In Matt 9:37, Jesus reminded his followers that "the workers are few" even where "the harvest is plentiful"—As a consequence, wild fruit is usually ignored. The "wild" oranges simply fall to the ground where they are eaten by animals and where a few seeds germinate in the soil to produce more wild trees.

Paul identified the "better" olive tree with the special relationship that existed between God and Israel and the "wild" olive tree with the non-Jewish people of the world. For the two thousand years between Abraham and the birth of Christ, God's holy root had been nurturing the Jewish branches of that good olive tree. During that time the Gentile nations were like wild olive trees growing out in the fields. They were strangers to God's covenant with Israel and isolated from the blessings of Rom 9:4–5.

The Bible says God entered into a special *covenant with Israel* and that he was pursuing a grand strategy that would eventually encompass the whole world. He had chosen or designated Israel not only "as a covenant to the [Jewish] people" but also as "a light to the [Gentile] nations" (Isa 42:6). Simeon understood God's general strategy when he saw the Christ child and said, "For my eyes have seen Thy salvation, Which Thou hast prepared in the presence of all peoples, a light of revelation to the Gentiles, And the glory of Thy people Israel" (Luke 2:32). The prophetess

Anna also associated Jesus' visit to the temple with "those who were looking for the redemption of Jerusalem" (Luke 2:36–38).

Paul's olive tree illustration shows that the *"new covenant"* included Jews, like Paul, but that it also included non-Jews like Luke. That is, God had grafted wild branches onto the cultivated olive tree. The apostle explained God's strategy when he said "some" of the branches from the cultivated tree were cut off and destroyed, and "some" of the branches from the wild tree were "grafted" onto the domesticated tree. Indeed, ". . . if some of the [Jewish] branches were broken off and you [non-Jews], being a wild olive, were grafted in *among* them and became partaker *with* them of the rich root of the olive tree, do not be arrogant toward the branches; but if you are arrogant, remember that it is not you who supports the root, but the root supports you" (Rom 11:17–18).

Parenthetically, I would add that Paul's denunciation of Gentile "arrogance" against the Jews in Rom 11:18 and 25 is clearly a condemnation of the anti-Semitism that has sometimes been visited upon Jews individually and collectively.

Generally, the Christian tradition views the breaking off of the domesticated olive branches as a reference to Israel that is both collective and individual. That is, the "breaking off" is a comprehensive indictment against all of the previously mentioned categories of Israel except for the Messianic Jews who have embraced the new covenant.

Many Christians view Israel's response to Christ through an all-or-nothing prism. For some, Israel's collective rejection of Jesus as Messiah has led them to adopt the doctrine of secessionism (or replacement theology) as mentioned in the previous chapter. This scenario suggests a doctrine where God is finished with all of Israel except for the Messianic Jews who have accepted the new covenant.

For others, Israel's collective rejection of Jesus, the scattering of the Jews in the Diaspora, and the reconstitution of the State of Israel in 1948 has led them to adopt a dispensational scenario in which a military and socio-political Israel will eventually result in a mass conversion to the new covenant, thus confirming their understanding of Paul's statement that, "all Israel will be saved" (Rom 11:26).

However, both perspectives fail to distinguish between collective Israel and individual Jews, and they interpret Paul's statement that *"all Israel will be saved"* as if it is related to a military/socio-political Israel where "all *Messianic Jews* will be saved."

Christianity and the Outsider

I find great irony in most of Christianity's end-times scenarios. I keep remembering that the Israelites misinterpreted the prophecies regarding Christ's First Advent because they were looking for a military and/or socio-political Messiah. I wonder if Christianity is making the same kind of mistake regarding Christ's Second Advent.

The difficulties involved in distinguishing between Israel's *collective* category and the *individuals* within that category can be seen in most families. On one hand, a "good" family can have a renegade son who is a disgrace to the whole family. On the other hand, a "bad" family can have a daughter who rises above her difficult circumstances. Paul minimized the importance of collective categories like Jewish or Gentile when he said, "Circumcision is nothing, and uncircumcision is nothing, but what matters is the keeping of the commandments of God" (1 Cor 7:18–19).

Jesus, himself, used the "branch" metaphor to refer to individuals when he said, "I am the vine and you are the branches; he who abides in Me . . . bears much fruit . . . If anyone does not abide in Me, he is thrown away as *a* branch, and dries up; and they gather them . . . and they are burned" (John 15:5–6). These "branches" refer to the fact that some individuals produce fruit and others do not. The branch metaphor was also used in the Old Testament to identify the coming Messiah as the individual "shoot" or "branch" that would "spring from the stem of Jesse."[1]

Paul was unequivocal in his Rom 9:1–6 indictment against *collective* Israel. But was he saying that all *individual* Jews are eternally estranged from God by virtue of Judaism's collective response to the Christ event— a response that Paul would eventually describe as providential (Rom 11:30–32)?

I am suggesting that Paul's discussion of the "branches" beginning in Rom 11:16 refers to the personal salvation of *any* individual whether Jewish or non-Jewish. In other words, the idea of cutting off "natural branches" or grafting them back later refers to the personal belief or unbelief of individual Jews rather than Israel's *collective rejection* of the new covenant. Similarly, the idea of grafting "wild branches" on the good olive tree or later cutting them off refers to the personal belief or unbelief of non-Jewish individuals rather than Christianity's *collective acceptance* of the new covenant.

---

1. See Isa 11:1, 53:2 and Jer 23:5.

Paul's Olive Tree: Insiders and Outsiders on the Same Tree?

The fact is that Paul's exposition does not say that *all* of the "natural branches" had been broken off the domesticated olive tree. Rather, he said "*some* of the [natural Jewish] branches were broken off" and *some* "wild olive" [non-Jewish] branches were "grafted *in among*" the natural [Jewish] branches and "became partaker *with* them" in the holy root of the good olive tree (Rom 11:17).

It should be noted that Paul's sentence structure juxtaposes belief and unbelief like the opposite sides of a coin. Like a rejoinder to a question, Rom 11:20 says, "Quite right, they were broken off for their unbelief (*apistia*), and you stand only by your faith (*pistis*)." We know he was talking about opposite sides of the same issue because both *pistis* and *apistia* are based on the same Greek root. *Pistis* has a positive meaning where one is "believing or faithful," but it takes the negative meaning of "unbelieving or unfaithful" when the prefix "*a*" is added to create *apistia*.

Paul said those first covenant branches were broken off because of their unbelief/unfaith *(apistia)*, and some non-covenant branches were grafted in because of their belief/faith *(pistis)*. The clear implication of the olive tree passage is that *some* first covenant "branches" remained on the tree along with the new covenant "branches" that were grafted on. So the root is simultaneously supporting both first covenant "branches" and new covenant "branches." Furthermore, the apostle used the same language regarding the branches on both sides of the tree. That is, in Rom 11:17–20, he spoke of Jewish branches being broken off and non-Jewish branches being grafted in—then he reversed the analogy by indicating in Rom 11:21–23 that non-Jewish branches could also be cut off and the Jewish branches could be grafted back onto the olive tree.

The issue then, is whether it really is all or nothing for Israel. Is Paul saying all Jewish *individuals* are "cut off" from the Son's atonement and the Father's forgiveness, except for the Messianic Jews? Is their loss the result of Judaism's *collective* rejection of the new covenant, or is there more to the story?

Intellectual honesty requires that Bible students apply the same standard to both sides of the olive tree. Therefore, we must ask, if Paul or anyone else would suggest that all *individual* Gentiles have been "grafted" into an "eternal inheritance" because of Christendom's collective acceptance of the new covenant. I think not! Therefore, one should not assume that all *individual* Jews have been "broken off" from the eternal inheritance merely because of Judaism's collective rejection of the new covenant. Indeed, it appears that in recent years, collective Christendom may be falling into the same pattern of unbelief that plagued collective Israel in former times.

Nature provides plenty of examples where plants or trees are grafted together and then continue to grow as one. I can remember seeing lemons growing on one side of a citrus tree and oranges growing on the other side. The root had produced lemon branches, the grafting process had produced orange branches, and the same tree was simultaneously producing two different kinds of fruit. Both sides of the tree were subject to the destructive forces of drought and disease, just as both first covenant and new covenant individuals are subject to the destructive effects of the sin nature.

Furthermore, the caretaker's job is the same on both sides of the tree. He has to cultivate the fruit bearing branches on both sides and prune and burn the deadwood from both sides—just as God's strategy eliminates some branches and grafts other branches onto Paul's olive tree. Maybe that old olive tree is big enough and strong enough to accommodate first covenant and new covenant branches simultaneously.

THE REMNANT OF PARTIALLY HARDENED INDIVIDUALS

The question is whether a faithful *remnant* of "first covenant" individuals has continued to exist within Judaism over the years, and whether that remnant can co-exist on the olive tree alongside the "new covenant" followers of Jesus Christ. Only God knows for sure whether Paul's two-in-one olive tree now has first covenant branches *and* new covenant branches growing on the same tree, but spiritual integrity requires that Christians should at least be open to the possibility of a continuing first covenant remnant.

Paul was focusing attention on the first covenant remnant when he referred to the "partial hardening that has happened to Israel" during the Gentile era, and then tied the partial hardening to the eventual salvation of the faithful remnant (Rom 11:25–26). Did this "partial hardening" refer to *collective* Israel's failure to participate in the new covenant, or was Paul talking about an *individual* Jew's response to God? Clearly, he was talking about individual Jews because he said some are hardened (Rom

11:7) but some are only partially hardened (Rom 11:25). Furthermore, it is entirely understandable that some first covenant insiders would continue to respond to God within the initial covenant, while others would respond to the new covenant.

What did Paul understand about God's remnant when he said:

> I say then, God has not rejected His people, has He? May it never be! . . . In the same way then, there has also come to be at the present time a *remnant* according to God's gracious *choice* . . . That which [collective] Israel is seeking for, it has not obtained, but those [individuals] who were *chosen* obtained it, and the rest [of the individuals] were hardened . . . For I do not want you, [non-Jewish] brethren to be uninformed of this mystery, lest you be wise in your own estimation, that a partial hardening has happened to Israel until the fulness of the Gentiles has come in; and thus all Israel will be saved; . . . From the standpoint of the gospel they [the first covenant remnant] are enemies for your sake, but from the standpoint of God's *choice* they are beloved for the sake of the fathers; for the gifts and the calling of God are irrevocable (Rom 11:5, 7, 25–26, 28–29).

Depending upon Israel's relationship to the eternal inheritance and whether individuals lived before or after the cross, Paul divided Jewish individuals into four groups:

First, there was a group of faithful Jews before the cross who obtained the eternal inheritance; ". . . those who were chosen *obtained it*" (Rom 11:7b). Second, there is a group of unfaithful Jews, whether before or after the cross, who are "hardened" and eternally separated from God. The first group obtained the inheritance, but ". . . the rest were *hardened*" (Rom 11:7c). Third, there is a contradictory group of chosen Jews after the cross. They are part of Judaism's rejection of the new covenant, but Paul said they are only "partially hardened." That is, "a partial hardening has happened to Israel *until* the fullness of the Gentiles has come in" (Rom 11:25). The fourth group contains faithful Jews like Peter and Paul, and all the other Messianic Jews who have embraced the new covenant since the cross.

The first, second, and fourth groups are rather straightforward. The first and second categories create an "either/or" situation where some Jews obtain the "eternal inheritance" and others do not. On one hand, the "children of the promise" are descendants and entitled to the inheritance;

on the other hand, the "children of the flesh" are not even to be regarded as descendants (Rom 9:8). Paul said, "For they are not all Israel who are descended from Israel; neither are they all children because they are Abraham's descendants" (Rom 9:6–8). A claim to the eternal inheritance by a person in the second group would be like a stranger showing up at my funeral and claiming an interest in my estate as if he were one of my children. Of course, the Messianic Jews in the fourth group are privy to the new covenant with all its benefits and responsibilities.

The third group, however, is problematic. It is made up of traditional Jews who must be viewed from two different perspectives. From the standpoint of the gospel, they are *enemies* because they are ethnic Jews who are part of collective Israel's rejection of the Messiah. However, the apostle also said ". . . from the standpoint of God's choice they are *beloved* for the sake of the fathers; for the gifts and the calling of God are irrevocable" (Rom 11:28–29).

GOOD NEWS AND BAD NEWS

The collective scenario is bad news for Israel because it says, "That which [collective] Israel is seeking for, it has not obtained . . . " (Rom 11:7a). However, the individual scenario contains both good news and bad news. The good news is that the "chosen" *obtained it* (Rom 11:7b), and the bad news is that the "the rest were hardened" and *did not obtain it* (Rom 11:7c). So who are the "chosen"?

The verb *poroo* (hardened) in Rom 11:7 and the noun *porosis* (hardening) in Rom 11:25 are both derived from *poros,* which means the "hardness" of a piece of rock. Figuratively speaking, *poroo* and *porosis* refer to people who are insensitive, blind, or "hardened" to God's redemptive purpose. Paul said collective Israel as well as the hardened individuals did not find what they were looking for, that is, an eternal inheritance. The indictment in Rom 11:7c is particularly devastating because it means the hardening is total and permanent.

However, Paul softened the charge against some individual Jews because he said the "chosen" of Rom 11:7b were only partially hardened. Indeed, the hardening is not only partial but also temporary. That is, "a *partial* hardening has happened to Israel *until* the fullness of the Gentiles

Paul's Olive Tree: Insiders and Outsiders on the Same Tree?

has come in; and thus all [of chosen] Israel will be saved; just as it is written" (Rom 11:25–26).

The total "hardening" of verse seven refers to Jewish individuals who were "broken off" the olive tree because of unbelief. The "partial hardening" of verse twenty-five refers to faithful first covenant Jews who remain on the olive tree in spite of their failure to embrace the new covenant. In other words, the "chosen" obtained the eternal inheritance because they were only the *partially hardened*, but the *totally hardened* (the rest) did not obtain it.

Regarding the future, Paul indicated that if Jewish individuals "... do not continue in their unbelief [or hardening]," they can be grafted back onto the olive tree, just as the non-Jewish wild branches were initially grafted onto the tree. Furthermore, the Gentiles are at risk for being broken off the olive tree even though they are privy to the new covenant because "if God did not spare the natural branches, neither will He spare you [wild branches] (Rom 11:20, 23–25, 20).

What should we make of the paradoxical Jews who are described as both "beloved" and "enemies" in Rom 11:28, and how are they related to God's remnant? I realize that many Christians identify the *remnant* of Israel in Rom 11:5 with the Messianic Jews who have accepted the new covenant. However, I would contend that the remnant cannot be limited to Messianic Jews because this "remnant" must include the "enemies" of the gospel who are "beloved" for the sake of the fathers (Rom 11:28), and Messianic Jews are not enemies of the gospel.

CONNECTING THE OLD AND NEW REMNANTS

Paul reached the climax of the Romans 9–11 argument when he said, "From the standpoint of the gospel they [the remnant] *are enemies* for your sake, but from the standpoint of God's choice they *are beloved* for the sake of the fathers" (Rom 11:28).

Admittedly, the apostle was disappointed that collective Israel had rejected the new covenant, and he was especially conflicted for the faithful individuals who were caught up in the process. But he continued to insist that, "God has not rejected his [chosen] people whom He foreknew. Or do you not know what the Scripture says in the passage about Elijah, how he pleads with God against Israel" (Rom 11:2)?

Paul seems to have used chapter 11 of Romans to connect the "old school" and the "new school"—that is, linking the New Testament remnant to Elijah's Old Testament remnant. Furthermore, his new remnant seems to contain the "enemies" of the gospel (Rom 11:28) as well as the Messianic Jews who have consciously embraced the gospel.

Recalling Elijah's experience after Mt. Carmel, Paul reminded his readers that there were faithful Jews at that time who had not "bowed the knee" to false gods. He said, "In the same way then, there has also come to be at the present time a *remnant* according to God's gracious choice" (Rom 11:5).

The apostle continued identifying the new remnant throughout chapter 11. In verse five the remnant is "according to God's gracious *choice*," and in verse seven they are "those who were *chosen*." If we stop our analysis at this point, we might conclude that these references to the "chosen" are limited to the Messianic Jews who have accepted the gospel of Jesus Christ. However, verse twenty-eight identifies the New Testament remnant as containing people who are *both* "beloved" of God *and* "enemies" of the gospel!

It would be absurd to suggest that the apostle Paul has somehow characterized Messianic Jews as "enemies" of the gospel. These Jews, including the apostle himself, have embraced Jesus as Israel's long awaited Messiah, and they have adopted the new covenant. To identify these people as "enemies" of the gospel would be a *non sequitur*—"It does not follow." Messianic Jews cannot be enemies of the gospel because they magnify the gospel!

On the contrary, Paul seems to be saying that some first covenant Jews (the faithful remnant) are *beloved*, notwithstanding their *enemy status* for having participated in collective Israel's collective rejection of the Messiah. So how are we to construe this "beloved/enemy" category?

Individually, the chosen are "beloved" because the "gifts and the calling" of the first covenant are "irrevocable." However, they are also "enemies" because they are part of *collective* Judaism and therefore identified with Judaism's providential rejection of the new covenant (Rom 11:25, 28–29).

The distinction seems to follow the *hardening* mentioned in verse seven and the *partial hardening* mentioned in verse twenty-five. The first covenant's rejection of the new covenant is manifested in Judaism's collective rejection of Jesus as the Messiah of Israel—"That which Israel was seeking for, it has not obtained" (Rom 11:7).

Collectively, there has been a *total rejection* of God's plan of redemption. However, for the remnant, there is only a *partial rejection*; that is, "a partial hardening" that will continue until "the fullness of the Gentiles has come in . . . " (Rom 11:25).

ISRAEL'S PROVIDENTIAL REJECTION OF JESUS

God was not surprised by collective Judaism's rejection of the new covenant:

Collectively, God's overall purpose was providential in that he was making redemption available both to Jews and non-Jews. Israel's collective disobedience was part of God's strategic plan to make reconciliation available to the whole world.

Individually, the enigma of faithful Jews being both "beloved" for the sake of the fathers and "enemies" of the gospel was and is part of a divine mystery, and Paul cautioned Gentiles against showing their ignorance regarding the matter. The "partial hardening" of first covenant "saints" in verse twenty-five is the individual aspect of collective Israel's providential rejection of the new covenant. Paul admitted that even God's chosen remnant had stumbled, but they "did not stumble so as to fall . . . But by their transgression salvation has come to the Gentiles . . . For if their rejection be the reconciliation of the world, what will their acceptance be but life from the dead? . . . For God has shut up all in disobedience that He might show mercy to all" (Rom 11:11–12, 15, 30–32).

In other words, the "gracious choice," "chosen," "beloved," "enemies" of verses five, seven, and twenty-eight obtained the eternal inheritance they were seeking, (Rom 11:5, 7, and 28) even though they will be *partially hardened* "until the fullness of the Gentiles has come in" (Rom 11: 25).

Paul's statements that "God has not rejected His people whom he foreknew" (Rom 11:2) and that "all Israel will be saved" (Rom 11:26) are less ambiguous if one understands that the remnant is made up of "Messianic Jews" as well as the "beloved enemies" of the gospel. Although "partially hardened" from a *collective* perspective, these chosen *individuals* are beloved even though they are privy only to the earlier covenant.

Christianity and the Outsider

THE RELATIONSHIP BETWEEN THE OLD AND NEW COVENANTS

In chapters 9 through 11 of Romans, Paul was dealing with complex issues involving both the first covenant and the new covenant:

From one perspective, the apostle's discussion had to address the difference between *faithful* Jews and the *unfaithful* Jews who are completely "hardened" to God's will (Rom 11:7). Paul said the hardened individuals should not even be referred to as Israel (Rom 9:6).

From another perspective, Paul had to address the divine mystery regarding the faithful remnant's response to the Christ event. On one hand, they are God's "chosen," and "the gifts and the calling of God are irrevocable" (Rom 11:28–29). On the other hand, they are "partially hardened" and therefore "enemies" of the gospel (Rom 11:25, 28).

How do we know that the "partial hardening" of the chosen has a temporary connotation instead of a permanent condemnation like the rest who were "hardened"? Paul made it clear that the partial hardening within Israel would continue only until the "fullness of the Gentiles has come in" (Rom 11:25).

No serious student of the Bible would suggest that the "fullness of the Gentiles" means that God's gift of eternal life is given to *individual* Gentiles merely because they are part of Christendom's *collective* or cultural acceptance of the new covenant. Therefore, no serious student of the Bible should suggest that the "partial hardening that has happened to Israel" means that God rejects all *individual* Jews merely because of Israel's *collective* or cultural rejection of the new covenant.

Cultural Israel's connection to the first covenant is not salvific—just as cultural Christianity's connection to the new covenant is not salvific. On the contrary, one's personal relationship with God is conditioned upon what Jesus called "repentance for forgiveness" (Luke 24:47, also see Luke 3:3).

Paul acknowledged the difference between the *collective* nature of divine providence and *individual* accountability when he cautioned Christians against arrogance and conceit. Speaking of the kindness and severity of God, he said, ". . . if God did not spare the natural [Jewish] branches, neither will He spare you [non-Jews] . . . And they [the Jewish branches] also, if they do not continue in their unbelief *(apistia)*, will be grafted in; for God is able to graft them in again (Rom 11:20–24).

Paul's Olive Tree: Insiders and Outsiders on the Same Tree?

Whereas God's collective providence is *irreversible*, the process of cutting off some individuals and grafting others onto the "olive tree" is *reversible* depending upon the belief or unbelief of the individual, and it doesn't matter whether that person is Jewish or non-Jewish.

Furthermore, as a former citrus grower, I can testify to the fact that grafting is not a collective process. It is a complex horticultural procedure that must be done one branch at a time—just as individuals respond to God one person at a time.

A few years ago I attended the funeral of a godly woman. Her son gave a moving eulogy, recounting how he had flown to Atlanta the day before the funeral. He said he rented a car at the airport, and stopped by the hometown church on his way to his motel. As he got out of his car, he was confronted with an open grave and realized, immediately, that it had been prepared for his mother's burial the next day.

With the passage of time, I have forgotten all the wonderful things he said about his mother that day, but burned into my memory, as if with a branding iron, is his statement that his mother's death became more real to him when he was faced with *"the reality of the hole"*!

The point is that we are born as individuals, we respond to God as individuals, and we die as individuals. The collective "faith of our fathers," whether Jewish, Christian, or otherwise, has providential significance in God's strategic plan for reconciling the world to himself, but those collective covenants are irrelevant when the individual is faced with "the reality of the hole."

The biblical covenants were and are *collective* vehicles. The first covenant emphasized the law and humanity's accountability to God, while the new covenant is focused on God's plan of redemption. Furthermore, Paul says the collective exclusion of Gentiles from the first covenant and the collective exclusion of Judaism from the new covenant were part of God's preordained plan to redeem all repentant people from their sinful imperfection (Rom 11:11–12, 30–32).

The ultimate reality is that one's relationship with God is a *personal* matter. Individual Jews are personally accountable to God whether they lived before or after the cross, and some are faithful *(pistos)* like Elijah and the apostle Paul while others are unfaithful *(apistia)* like King Ahab and Judas Iscariot. Likewise, non-Jewish individuals are accountable to God whether they lived before or after the cross, and some are faithful *(pistos)* like Abel and Luke while others are unfaithful *(apistia)* like Cain

Christianity and the Outsider

and Pontius Pilate. One thing is sure—There is no partiality with God (Rom 2:11).

The first covenant was broadened from Abraham's immediate family, to the twelve tribes, to Israel as a nation, to the Diaspora, and now to modern Judaism and the State of Israel. The spread of the "first covenant" seems to have been a precursor to the expansion of the "new covenant" from the disciples, to the early church in Israel, to non-Jews in the surrounding lands, to the Orthodox and Roman Catholic traditions, to Protestantism, and all the other Christian groups located in cultures around the world.

Having ethnic connections to the first covenant or cultural connections to the new covenant are important because they are part of God's overall plan of redemption. However, mere participation in these collective covenants should not be interpreted as personal salvation. The apostle Paul actually played down the importance of spiritual achievements or "works" when he said, "If any man's work which he has built upon it [Christ as the foundation] remains, he shall receive a reward. If any man's work is burned up, he shall suffer loss; but he himself shall be saved, yet so as through fire" (1 Cor 3:15).

The author of Hebrews spoke of a personal relationship with God when he said, ". . . without faith it is impossible to please Him, for he who comes to God must believe that He is, and that He is a rewarder of those who seek Him" (Heb 11:6).

Whether viewed as operating retrospectively *(paresis)* or prospectively *(aphesis)*, the atonement of Jesus Christ dramatizes the fact that having a relationship with God is a personal issue for each individual. As the saying goes, "God has children, but he has no grandchildren." However, if personal salvation is not perfected through the biblical covenants or by having "faith *in* Jesus Christ," then how does one come into right relationship with God?

18

From Accountability to Repentance to Forgiveness

> What does it mean for an individual to have a "personal relationship with God," and how is repentance related to personal accountability and divine forgiveness?

PERSONAL ACCOUNTABILITY

As discussed earlier, the idea of a perfect God having a personal relationship with imperfect human beings is inherent in the Judeo-Christian message. However, the message also requires personal accountability. Indeed, if eternity does not hold Adolph Hitler accountable for his atrocities, then the distinction between Hitler and Mother Teresa is of limited consequence.

As Israel's greatest ruler, King David had his own accountability in mind when he said, "The sacrifices of God are a broken spirit. A broken and contrite heart, O God, Thou wilt not despise" (Ps 51:17). David knew God was interested in personal brokenness rather than pious rituals and other religious activities.

The prophecy of Jeremiah reinforced the idea of individual accountability. The prophet said there would come a time when people would no longer speak of children's teeth being "set on edge" because the fathers had "eaten sour grapes . . . But every one will die for his own iniquity; each man who eats the sour grapes, his teeth will be set on edge" (Jer 31:29, 30).

Ezekiel also spoke of personal accountability when he said: "'As I live,' declares the Lord God, 'you are surely not going to use this proverb [children's teeth set on edge] in Israel any more. Behold, all souls are mine . . . The soul who sins will die . . . Therefore I will judge you, O house of Israel, *each* according to his conduct,' declares the Lord God. 'Repent and turn away from all your transgressions, so that iniquity may not become a stumbling block to you. Cast away from you all your transgressions which you have committed, and make yourselves a new heart and a new spirit . . . *repent* and live'" (Ezek 18:3–4, 30–32).

What about the personal accountability of non-Jews? The story of Job seems to predate God's covenant relationship with Israel. Even back then, Job's climactic affirmation was, "I have heard of Thee by the hearing of the ear; But *now* my eye sees Thee; Therefore I retract, And I *repent* in dust and ashes" (Job 42:5–6).

The story of Jonah is sometimes described as the greatest fish tale ever told. But the real significance of the story is that non-Jews were being reminded that they, too, were accountable for sin. Israel's reluctant prophet preached repentance to a Gentile nation—"Then the people of Nineveh believed in God; and they called a fast and put on sackcloth from the greatest to the least of them . . . When God saw their deeds, that they *turned* [repented] from their wicked way, then God relented concerning the calamity which He had declared He would bring upon them" (Jonah 3:5, 10).

It should be noted, however, that God's special relationship with Israel was not in play in the story of Nineveh. That is, the non-covenant people of Nineveh responded to God as individuals, but there was no conversion to Judaism. *Individually*, they repented, but *collectively*, they continued their non-covenant status. The Scripture even alludes to Nineveh's non-covenant position by indicating that Nineveh was spiritually ignorant regarding the ways of God. The text says the people did not know ". . . the difference between their right and left hand" (Jonah 4:11). Nevertheless, God showed compassion because the people of Nineveh responded to him with what King David described as "broken and contrite" hearts.

PERSONAL REPENTANCE

Between the Old and New Testaments, there was a silence that lasted over four hundred years. Then the gospel writers and other apostolic messengers began to focus on the importance of repentance:

> John the Baptist said, "*Repent*" (Matt 3:2)!
> Jesus said, "*Repent*" (Matt 4:17)!
> Peter, the leader of the twelve, said, "*Repent*" (2Pet 3:9)!
> And Paul, the apostle to the Gentiles, said, "*Repent*" (Acts 26:20)!

The Scripture says John the Baptist came out of the wilderness "preaching a baptism of *repentance for forgiveness*" (Luke 3:3). And Jesus, himself, confirmed the connection between repentance and forgiveness when he said, "Thus it is written, that the Christ should suffer and rise again from the dead the third day; and that *repentance for forgiveness* of sins should be proclaimed in His name to all the nations, beginning from Jerusalem" (Luke. 24:46–47).

In Romans 1, the apostle Paul said, "The wrath of God is revealed from heaven against *all* . . . unrighteousness of men" (Rom 1:18), but in Romans 2 he emphasized the "kindness and forbearance and patience" of God and stated that "the kindness of God leads *(ago)* us to repentance" (Rom 2:4). Indeed, God's "wrath" and "kindness" in Romans 1 and 2 parallel the "kindness" and "severity" of God in Rom 11:22–23 where the apostle explained divine providence in terms of the kindness and severity applicable to both Jews and Gentiles.

Paul used "wrath" *(orge)* to indicate God's abhorrence of sin, but then used "leads" *(ago)* to show that God entices sinners towards repentance without forcing his will upon them. Paul's use of the word *ago* is particularly significant because it means, "to bring, to entice, to lead gently and without violence." Like the prodigal son and the father in Luke 15, a sinner is confronted with the barrenness of his rebellion, but the Father does not force his will upon the rebellious sinner. The sinner either surrenders his own will or continues rebelling against the Father's will.

Augustine, perhaps the greatest of the early church fathers, reaffirmed the divine enticement when he said, "Thou madest [created] us for Thyself, and our heart is restless [accountable to thee] until it repose in Thee."[1] Apparently, there is something within us that draws us towards

---

1. Augustine, *The Confession of Saint Augustine*, 11.

repentance, yet we are not programmed to react like mindless robots. The situation is like the old saying, "You can lead a horse to water, but you can't make him drink!" God leads us toward repentance, but, like the prodigal son's father, he does not force his will upon us.

Paul concluded the Romans 9 through 11 argument with a statement that shows God used Israel's collective disobedience as part of a providential strategy for drawing both covenant and non-covenant individuals to himself—"For just as you [Gentiles] once were disobedient to God but now have been shown mercy because of their disobedience, so these [Jews] also now have been disobedient, in order that because of the mercy shown to you they also may now be shown mercy. For God has shut up *all* in disobedience that He might show mercy to *all*" (Rom 11:30–32). As mentioned earlier, God was not surprised by Israel's collective disobedience because it was part of his plan to provide deliverance to covenant insiders as well as outsiders.

So what does it mean, "to repent"? Is repentance a theological doctrine that applies only to religious insiders who are privy to God's special covenants? Or did the sovereign God of the universe create a plan where *all* people are free, but where *each* person is accountable to God for his freedom, especially freedom's vulnerability to pride. As individuals, all people are accountable to God for their sin, and God leads everyone toward repentance, but each person is free to repent or to rebel.

Linguistically, the Greek terms *melo*, *metamelomai*, and *metanoeo* suggest a progressive mindset regarding repentance, and they are applicable to covenant insiders as well as non-covenant outsiders:

1. *Melo* is a primary verb that means "to care" or "to be interested" in something. We "care" about things that are important to us. I am reminded of Arthur Miller's play *Death of a Salesman* where a nondescript salesman named Willie Loman had died, and his life was being belittled. Responding to the disrespect, Willie's defiant wife declared, "Attention must be paid." Her husband's life had meaning, and she wanted people to "care" about him.[2]

2. *Metamelomai* is a compound verb using *meta* (afterward) as the prefix and *melo* (to care) as the root. The literal meaning is "to care afterwards." The compounded word means to "regret" the

---

2. Miller, *Death of a Salesman*, 40.

consequences of one's act. The malefactor regrets that he got caught, but it is conceivable that he might stage a repeat performance if he can figure a way to avoid the unpleasant outcome.

3. *Metanoeo* is another compound verb that uses *meta* (afterward) as a prefix, but the new root is *noeo*, which means "to exercise the mind *(nous)*, to think, to perceive, to understand." When compounded, the new word continues the idea of thinking-afterwards, but mere "regret" *(metamelomai)* has evolved into "repentance" *(metanoia)*, which is a radical change of heart. Repentance is not merely a personality adjustment or "turning over a new leaf." With repentance, the old self with its pride and its self-righteousness has died.

A youthful misadventure involving my father and an older brother demonstrates the spiritual difference between the repentance of *metanoeo* and the regret of *metamelomai*. It seems that they had been rather rowdy and had spent the night in jail. The next morning my dad assured the judge that he had learned his lesson and that he wouldn't be back in court, and he never was—*metanoeo!* However, his older brother was the family adventurer who was always testing the limits of authority. When the judge asked whether he would ever be back in court, he said he didn't know—*metamelomai!*

Repentance brings a new perspective like the attitude that was in Christ, himself. According to Paul, Christ "existed in the form of God, [but] did not regard equality with God a thing to be grasped, but emptied Himself . . . He humbled Himself by becoming obedient to the point of death, even death on a cross" (Phil 2:5–8). With personal repentance, the old attitude is not something to be "grasped" and held onto. Rather, the repentant sinner is emptied of pride and self-righteousness and humbled to the point of spiritual death.

Spiritually speaking, repentance means the restless sinner has faced the eternal abyss and realized his inadequacy before the God of the universe. The natural man is spiritually dead, but with the sinner's repentance and the Father's forgiveness, the spiritual man is resurrected to new life.

CONNECTING REPENTANCE AND FORGIVENESS

What is the connection between human *repentance* and divine *forgiveness*? Paul made it clear that the connecting link is the *atonement* of Jesus Christ:

> But God demonstrated His own love to us, in that while we were yet sinners, Christ died for us. Much more then, having now been justified by His blood [atonement], we shall be saved from the wrath of God through Him. For if, while we were enemies, we were reconciled to God through the death of His Son, much more, having been reconciled, we shall be saved by His life . . . For if we have become united with Him in the likeness of His death, certainly we shall be also in the likeness of His resurrection, knowing this, that our old self was crucified with Him [repented], that our body of sin might be done away with [forgiven], that we should no longer be slaves to sin; for he who has died is free from sin (Rom 5:8–10, 6:4–7).

With repentance, the *natural man* is crucified with Christ. However, he is then justified by Christ through his atonement. Having been justified by the Son, the sinner becomes the *spiritual man,* who receives the Father's forgiveness, is resurrected to new life, and has "the mind of Christ" (1 Cor 2:14–16).

> The Sacred Link
> The sinner's *repentance* means spiritual death,
> The Son's *atonement* justifies the sinner, and
> The Father's *forgiveness* provides newness of life.

A sinner trying to avoid repentance is like a criminal running from the police. He jumps from rooftop to rooftop, but eventually, he approaches a gap that is higher and wider than anything he has seen before. Unable to save himself, he either surrenders to his pursuer or challenges the sovereignty of his pursuer.

In Francis Thompson's famous poem, "The Hound of Heaven," God, himself, pursues each restless soul like "the hound follows the hare." Responding to God's pursuit, some people empty themselves in repentance, and others continue their rebellion against God.

In another way, repentance is like a drowning man who tries to save himself by grabbing at flotsam or struggling with a lifeguard. Spiritually, repentance occurs when the "swimmer" realizes he cannot save himself

From Accountability to Repentance to Forgiveness

and goes down the third time to spiritual death; then the lifeguard can save him. Paul said, "I am crucified with Christ [I'm "dead"] nevertheless I live [I'm "alive"] . . . And the [temporal] life which I now live in the flesh I live by the faith *of* the Son of God, who loved me, and gave Himself for me" (Gal 2:20 KJV).

The "wages of sin" brings death (Rom 6:23a)—Repentance means fallen flesh has acknowledged spiritual death; the "natural man" is *dead*. However, "the *free gift* of God is eternal life in Christ Jesus our Lord" (Rom 6:23b)—So the resurrected "spiritual man" is *alive*. Whether it's Job in the Old Testament or the prodigal son in the New Testament, the natural man is helpless, and deliverance is not a factor without the repentance that acknowledges sinful imperfection and accepts spiritual death. However, the Son's atonement takes the blame for the sinner's imperfection, cleanses the sinner of unrighteousness, and opens the door to the Father's forgiveness.

I should mention, at this point, that repentance does not mean self-hate or some other behavioral trait dealing with chronic depression or low self esteem. Jesus said, "Love your neighbor *as* yourself," not *instead* of yourself (Matt 22:39). In terms of having a healthy mental attitude, nothing could be more uplifting than to realize that human beings are created in the image of God and that God-as-Son suffered and died to redeem the repentant sinner from his or her sinful imperfection.

HUMAN LIMITATIONS

Spiritual resurrection is not so much a *changed* heart as it is an *exchanged* heart—a spiritual heart transplant! With a medical transplant, there is a natural tendency for the recipient's immune system to reject the donor heart. Therefore, medical steps must be taken to avoid rejection of the new heart tissue. Spiritually speaking, there is a natural tendency to reject the spiritual heart transplant that is available through the "faith *of* Jesus Christ." Obviously, there is nothing wrong with the new "heart" that is made available through Christ's atonement. But the natural man rejects even the offer of a new heart unless repentance has caused the old man to be "crucified with Christ" (Gal 2:20).

The natural man is rather like a wild horse. The upside of being a wild horse is that it is free to roam and do as it pleases. The downside is that it is at risk to natural hazards like disease, storms, and predatory beasts. When a wild horse is brought into the corral, it loses its independence, but it gains the benefits of a new life. Even so, when a saddle is strapped on the horse, it bucks, kicks, and races in all directions, desperately trying to break free from the will of the trainer.

Once a horse has been "broken," it can never go back to being "unbroken." It may return to the wild and run with the herd, but it can never be an "unbroken" horse. The same principle applies to the "broken and contrite heart"—it can never go back to being an "unbroken" heart. A person who has surrendered to the sovereignty of God may return to some of his old ways, but he cannot "un-surrender" any more than one can "un-ring" a bell.

Some animals, including some "human animals," would rather die than submit to the will of the Master. In law enforcement, for example, some lawbreakers brag that they will never be "taken alive." Sometimes referred to as "suicide by cop," the boast often means a subject would rather die in a hail of bullets than surrender to governmental authority.

Spiritually speaking, when the kindness of God leads lawbreakers to repentance, some surrender, but others would rather die in their sin than surrender to divine authority (Rom 2:4–5). Up-lifted hands, of course, is the universal sign of surrender. True repentance, then, is the up-lifted hands of spiritual death. The natural man surrenders when he forfeits the pride and self-righteousness that are characteristic of human nature.

Admittedly, not everyone who says "Lord, Lord" has a broken and contrite heart, and sometimes it is difficult to distinguish between repentant sinners and imposters. Only God knows the difference between a broken spirit and an imposter, but scripture makes it clear that there will come a day of reckoning.

In Matthew 13 Jesus dedicated a whole parable to differentiating between believers and imposters. Using a wheat field as an analogy, he said it is impossible to tell the difference between the "wheat and the tares" (sons of the kingdom and the sons of the evil one) during the growing season. Furthermore, premature attempts to root out the weeds would do irreparable damage to the wheat. Jesus cautioned his followers that they should not concern themselves with separating the "wheat and the tares" and assured them that the "sons of the evil one" would be separated and cast out "in the day of final judgment." He said, "in the time of harvest I

From Accountability to Repentance to Forgiveness

will say to the reapers, 'First gather up the tares and bind them in bundles to burn them up; but gather the wheat into my barn'" (Matt 13:30).

Later, when Jesus was concluding his earthly ministry, he said, "And all the nations will be gathered before Him [the Son of Man], and He will separate them from one another, as the shepherd separates the sheep from the goats" (Matt 25:32–33).

Jesus even indicated there will be some surprises on that great judgment day: On one hand, the righteous will feel unworthy but be happy when the King says, "Come, you who are blessed of My Father, inherit the kingdom prepared for you from the foundation of the world" (Matt 25:34). On the other hand, some will claim a relationship with the Lord but be stunned to hear the King say, "Depart from Me accursed ones, into the eternal fire which has been prepared for the devil and his angels" (Matt 25:41).

As I mentioned in chapter 2, this final parable in Matthew's gospel shows no preference for either first covenant insiders or new covenant insiders. God's only measure is whether the righteous "insiders" were compassionate to society's outsiders, and he identified himself with the outsiders.

The fact that some covenant insiders may be excluded and some covenant outsiders may be included in heaven's "eternal inheritance" suggests that the final identification of the wheat and the tares will not be resolved until the end of the age. So what's the difference between the Christian insiders who respond to God's special revelation and the non-Christian outsiders who respond to God's general revelation?

KNOWING THAT WE KNOW

People who hear and respond to the gospel of Jesus Christ realize that they are privy to the new covenant, and they know they have been grafted onto the olive tree mentioned in chapter 11 of Romans. Indeed, 1 John 5:13 says, "These things I have written to you who believe in the name of the Son of God, in order that you may know *(eido)* that you have eternal life." First comes the "who" and then comes the "what"!

Who were the people John was addressing? He was writing to the family of believers as any father might write to his "little children" *(teknion). Teknion* is the diminutive form of child *(teknon)* and is used in this passage as a term of endearment. The master teacher was sharing a "family secret" with his disciples. This limited nature of the audience is clear from John's repeated use of the term "little children" in 1 John 2:1, 12, 28, 3:7, 18, 4:4, and 5:21.

And *what* was the teacher's message to his followers? He would certainly have agreed with Jesus' salvific statement in Luke 24:47 that "repentance for forgiveness of sins should be proclaimed" to all people. But John was adding a note of assurance. The new covenant means people not only have access to eternal life but can also *"know"* that they have eternal life—"These things have been written . . . in order that you may know *(eido)* that you have eternal life" (1 John 5:13). The literal meaning of *eido* is to see with your eyes, but the figurative meaning is "to see" or understand intuitively with your mind.

There is a sharp contrast, however, between knowing something intuitively as opposed to knowing something based on experience. For example, there is the intuitive *eido* of "knowing" the beauty of the Grand Canyon on your first visit as opposed to the experiential *ginosko* of "knowing" the taste of strawberry ice cream because you have tasted strawberry ice cream in the past.

The key to understanding general and special revelation is in realizing that John used both the intuitive knowledge of *eido* and the experiential knowledge of *ginosko* in the same verse (1 John 5:20). He began verse twenty by repeating the intuitive knowledge *(eido)* from verse thirteen. All sinners, including John's covenant insiders, are intuitive regarding their general accountability for sin. That is, the Spirit of God convicts all people of sin and leads them to repentance, and some repent while others rebel (Rom 2:4–5).

However, if the repentant sinner is privy to the new covenant, he also knows that the Son of God has come and that he has provided greater understanding. When the covenant insider repents, is forgiven, and finds himself at the foot of the cross, he knows intuitively *(eido)* that he has gone from death unto life (John 5:24 and 1 John 3:14). In other words, he knows *(eido)* the truth intuitively. But he is also in a position to finish verse twenty; that is, he can also ". . . know *(ginosko)* Him [experientially] who is true, and we are in Him who is true, in His Son Jesus Christ. This is the true God and eternal life" (1 John 5:20).

The Christian insider "experiences" *(ginosko)* God because God intervened in human history in the person of Jesus Christ. The fourth gospel says, "If you had known *(ginosko)* Me, you would have known *(ginosko)* My Father also; from now on you know *(ginosko)* Him, and have seen Him . . . He who has seen Me has seen the Father" (John 14:7–9). John says we *know God* experientially by virtue of the experience that is in and through Jesus Christ. But what does it mean to have a relationship in and through Christ?

Jesus existed in space-time as we do, and he had personal relationships with other people as we do. We love family and friends, so we can identify with his love for others and for his heavenly father. We have been tempted, so we can identify with his temptation. Most people have felt betrayed at some point and experienced some kind of suffering, so we can identify with his betrayal and suffering. Finally, we know that someday we are going to face the "reality of the hole," as mentioned earlier, and his victory over death authenticates the "blessed hope" that we, too, can have victory over death (Isa 25:8, 1 Cor 15:26, 55–58). His birth, death, and resurrection bridge the great gulf between time and eternity, and we are the beneficiaries who trust that we will also be able to cross that bridge.

1 John 5:20 says Christians insiders have the assurance of knowing the truth both intuitively *(eido)* and experientially *(ginosko)*: General revelation brings general accountability through the law and the intuitive knowledge *(eido)* that the Father holds everyone accountable for sin; therefore people either repent or rebel. Special revelation comes through the new covenant; therefore, insiders have experiential knowledge *(ginosko)* that the Son has come and that his atonement has made the Father's forgiveness available. In other words, as Christian insiders, *we know that we know*. The historical reality is that non-Christian outsiders are strangers to the new covenant, and they have to live without the assurance of *knowing that they know*—that is, without "knowing" God in the fullness of 1 John 5:20.

19

No Other Name Under Heaven

> In the past, Scripture passages such as "no one comes to the Father but through me" have meant that the Son's atonement is available only to covenant insiders through special revelation. However, if the Son is truly the constant Christ who is the same yesterday, today, and forever, then the benefits of his atonement could also be available to covenant outsiders through general revelation.

In this last chapter, I must address what most Christians view as the ultimate issue in any discussion of general revelation. I refer, of course, to the biblical passages that allegedly exclude non-Christians from the saving grace of Christ's atonement. Three of the most powerful references are:

1. "I am the way, and the truth, and the life; *no one comes to the Father, but through me*" (John 14:6).
2. "And there is salvation in *no one else;* for there is *no other name under heaven* that has been given among men, by which we must be saved" (Act 4:12).
3. "Truly, truly, I say to you, he who does not enter by the door into the fold of the sheep, but climbs up some other way, he is a thief and a robber . . . *I am the door;* if anyone enters through Me, he shall be saved, and shall go in and out, and find pasture" (John 10:1, 9).

However, Jesus went on to say, "And I have other sheep, which are *not* of this fold; I must bring them also, and they shall hear My voice; and they shall become one flock with one shepherd" (John 10:16). John added that Jesus' death was "not for the [Jewish] nation only, but that He might also gather together into one the [non-Jewish] children of God who are scattered abroad" (John 11:52).

Ironically, the exclusionary language that has always worked against general revelation may be its strongest point *when understood in the context of relativity theory.* As explained earlier, the Bible identifies the constant Christ of Heb 13:8 as the non-linear mediator between human uniformity and the non-uniformity of God—just as the constant speed of light in $E=mc^2$ mediates between uniform motion and non-uniform motion. If Christ is the non-linear mediator between God and humanity, he should also be thought of as the non-linear mediator between special revelation and general revelation—just as the constant speed of light mediates between special relativity and general relativity.

When revelation is understood as analogous to relativity, nothing changes with reference to the new covenant and the traditional understanding of special revelation. As a practical matter, most covenant insiders will continue to assume that Christ's atonement is a special remedy from sin, that is, limited to new covenant insiders. The problem is that recognizing Christ's special revelation for insiders and ignoring his general revelation for outsiders is like a bird that has to get by with one wing. It can function at the ground level, but it can never soar.

When revelation is understood in the full context of relativity theory, it not only recognizes humanity's general accountability for sin but also affirms Christ's atonement as a general remedy from sin. That is, the non-linear impact of the constant Christ brings an expanded Christology regarding general revelation. In this new context, the redemptive work of Jesus Christ is the same whether we are discussing the salvation of insiders who are privy to the new covenant (special revelation) or outsiders who have to live without the benefit of the new covenant (general revelation).

The limited scope of the linear perspective is somewhat analogous to society's continuing use of Newtonian physics as a *special* application of Einstein's *general* theory of relativity. Newtonian physics is useful at ground level, but if one wants to soar to the moon and beyond, he must use Einsteinian physics. Indeed, to paraphrase the prophet Isaiah, if we want to claim the whole world for the glory of God, we need to "mount up with wings" and soar like eagles (Isa 40:31).

Admittedly, the human perspective changes depending upon a person's time, place, and circumstances, but the constant Christ does not change. Therefore, I quote the so-called exclusionary passages with great confidence. Jesus really *is* the "door" and the "way, the truth, and the life," and there really *is* "no other name given among men" whereby a person can be redeemed from his or her imperfection. The same premise holds true for the other exclusionary Scriptures.

I will carry the argument a step further. If we pursue the various metaphors John's gospel uses to describe our relationship to God, we see the constant Christ as all inclusive:

> He is the *shepherd* who tends the "sheep" (John 10:11).
> He is the *living water* that quenches their thirst (John 4:10).
> He is the *bread of life* that satisfies their hunger (John 6:35).
> He is the *door* into the fold where they are safe (John 10:9).
> He is the *road* on which they walk (John 14:6).
> He is the *Word* they think (John 1:1–5, 14).
> He is the *light* that illumines their darkness (John 8:12).

At least seventy-five times in Paul's letters, he tells us that we are *"in Christo"* (in Christ). Like a bird is in the air or a fish is in the water, we are "in Christ." As the shepherd who leads the flock, Christ is our protector. He is the spiritual food and drink that sustains us. He is the road we travel, the door through which we enter the future, and the breath we breathe. He is the thought we think, and the light that dispels the darkness.

The Psalmist acknowledged God as the relentless hound of heaven when he said, "O Lord, Thou hast searched me and known me. Thou dost know when I sit down and when I rise up. Thou dost understand my thoughts from afar . . . Where can I go from Thy Spirit? Or where can I flee from Thy presence? If I ascend to heaven, Thou art there; If I make my bed in Sheol, behold, Thou art there; If I take the wings of the dawn, If I dwell in the remotest part of the sea, Even there Thy hand will lead me, and Thy right hand will lay hold of me" (Ps 139:1–2, 7–10).

No one can hide from God. And no one can avoid accountability to God. The power of God permeates every aspect of creation, and his Son's atonement reaches out in all directions, just as light radiates in all directions. It seems clear, therefore, that everyone knows *enough* to be accountable to God and *enough* to respond to God. And God has *enough* power to redeem anyone.

Admittedly, the human perspective is subject to the limitations of time and space. But God is not limited by time and space. He is not limited by the historicity of the Old and New Testaments, by the geography of the Holy Lands and Western Civilization, or by his special covenants with Israel and the Christian church.

It should be understood, therefore, that the light of revelation shines in all directions and can shine on anyone at anytime. Of course, some might say, if God's general revelation is able to save some non-Christians, what is the significance of Christianity, and what is so special about special revelation? Indeed, what is the advantage of being a Christian, and who is a true Christian?

Two thousand years ago, the apostle Paul struggled with the problem of Jewish identify, thus foreshadowing the contemporary problem of Christian identify. So who is a *true* Jew? Paul said:

> For when Gentiles [*non-Jews*] who do not have the *Law* do instinctively the things of the Law, these, not having the Law, are a law to themselves, in that they show the work of the Law written in their hearts . . . For he is not a *Jew* who is one outwardly . . . But he is a Jew who is one inwardly; and *circumcision* is that which is of the heart, by the Spirit, not by the letter; and His praise is not from men, but from God. Then what advantage has the Jew? Or what is the benefit of circumcision? Great in every respect . . . they were entrusted with the oracles of God (Rom 2:14–15, 28–29, 3:1–2).

So who is a *true* Christian? That was the question in the first century, and it is the question that haunts twenty-first century Christians. Paraphrasing the apostle Paul, I would say:

> For when *non-Christians* who do not have the *gospel* do instinctively the things of the gospel, these, not having the gospel, are a gospel to themselves, in that they show the work of the gospel written in their hearts . . . For he is not a *Christian* who is one outwardly . . . But he is a Christian who is one inwardly; and *baptism* is that which is of the heart, by the Spirit, not by the letter; and his praise is not from men, but from God. Then what advantage has the Christian? Or what is the benefit of baptism? Great in every respect . . . Christians have been entrusted with the oracles of God.

Christianity and the Outsider

Christians enjoy a confidence that grows out of being *privy* to the new covenant, and that should never be taken lightly. As mentioned earlier, "These things I have written to you who believe in the name of the Son of God, in order that you may *know* that you have eternal life (1 John 5:13). Such assurance is available only to covenant insiders who have called on his name.

People who are *not privy* to the new covenant live their lives in existential uncertainty, never knowing for sure whether they have received God's grace. I think the apostle Paul had these outsiders in mind on Mars Hill when he said; "perhaps they might grope for Him [God] and find Him" (Acts 17:27). Later, he went even further when he said, "If a man's work is burned up, he shall suffer loss, but he himself shall be saved" (1 Cor 3:15).

As believers, we would do well to remember Paul's caveat against Gentile hubris. "For I do not want you, brethren to be uninformed [or "ignorant" as the King James Version says] of this mystery, lest you be wise in your own estimation . . . " (Rom 11:25). Paul, himself, acknowledged humanity's limited capacity for understanding the providential relationship between the first covenant and the new covenant when he said, "Oh, the depth of the riches both of the wisdom and knowledge of God! How unsearchable are His judgments and unfathomable His ways" (Romans 11:33)!

20

Conclusion

The relativity model as set forth in *Christianity and the Outsider* makes it possible for contemporary people:

- To realize that the gospel story is real and personal, otherwise Christianity is an illusion,
- To appreciate the dignity of both insiders and outsiders, otherwise the justice championed by Jesus and the prophets of Israel is meaningless, and
- To acknowledge the connection between religion and science, otherwise there is no linkage between God as Creator and the physical world he created.

Isaiah was looking down the road to post-exile Israel when he said, "Enlarge the place of your tent; Stretch out the curtains of your dwellings, spare not; Lengthen your cords, and strengthen your pegs" (Isa 54:2). However, perhaps the time has come for contemporary Christianity to follow Isaiah's lead and to pitch a bigger tent.

Without demeaning or minimizing traditional Christology, the relativity model confirms personal *repentance* as the recognition of spiritual death and reaffirms the life-giving grace of God—as manifested in the Son's *atonement* and the Father's *forgiveness*. As the apostle Paul said, "And the Law came in that the transgression might increase, but where sin increased, grace abounded all the more, that, as sin reigned in death,

Christianity and the Outsider

even so grace might reign through righteousness to eternal life through Jesus Christ our Lord" (Rom. 5:20).

The Christ event should be understood as a tent that is large enough to accommodate both insiders and outsiders. Most insiders would acknowledge that insiders *and* outsiders are accountable to God ("all have sinned"). But for most insiders, the possibility of an outsider being reconciled with God would be unorthodox to say the least.

The transition from unorthodox ideas to orthodoxy is a well-traveled path. Before Christ, Israel's sacrificial system had been the exclusive domain of the Jews for over a thousand years. Following the Christ event, the spiritual tent was expanded to include the Messianic Jews who made up the early church.

The tent was then enlarged to include non-Jews as set forth in Acts 10 and 11, as well as Acts 13 and 14 where Peter, Paul, and others ministered to Gentiles in Joppa, Antioch, and Asia Minor. The inclusion of Gentiles in the new "way" became a major controversy in the early church. Indeed, the apostle Paul pointed out in Gal 2:11 that he had to oppose Peter "to his face" because Peter had sided with "the party of circumcision." These so-called Judaizers wanted to treat Gentiles as second-class Christians by forcing them to comply with the requirements of the Mosaic Law. Paul enlarged the tent by teaching that non-Jews were to have equal footing with Messianic Jews in the new covenant. The Jerusalem Conference in Acts 15 set the tone and helped open the door to Gentile participation in the early church and then throughout the Roman Empire.

With the fall of Rome, the western tent was farther extended as Christians evangelized Northern Europe, North America, and the rest of Western civilization. Over the years, Augustine, Thomas Aquinas, Martin Luther, John Calvin, and others continually re-energized Christianity and expanded its reach. The same expansion was taking place in the East where the Orthodox Church was reaching out to Asians and Eastern Europeans.

Now, Penn State professor Philip Jenkins is reporting in *The Next Christendom: The Coming of Global Christianity* that Christianity is once again experiencing a major transformation as it shifts from being primarily a Northern Hemisphere religion based in Europe and North American to a Southern Hemisphere religion focused in Asia, Africa, and South America. Culturally, the mostly white, upper-middle-class church of the

North is becoming predominately the black, brown, and Hispanic church of the South.[1]

Notwithstanding all the changes, the common denominator is the expanding Christology of the constant Christ. Indeed, the apostle Paul's familiar phrase, *"in Christo"* may be more profound and more inclusive than Christianity has realized. If "the just shall live by faith" could revolutionize European society and produce the Sixteenth Century Reformation, perhaps an understanding that the constant Christ is the "light of the world" can revolutionize today's global society and produce a twenty-first-century reformation that will shock today's church as thoroughly as the Protestant Reformation shocked the Roman Catholic Church.

Special revelation validates the *faith* of covenant insiders, general revelation provides *hope* for covenant outsiders, and the Christ event proves the *love* of God. "But now abide faith, hope, love; these three; but the greatest of these is love" (1 Cor 13:13).

---

1. Jenkins, *The Next Christendom*, 237–238.

APPENDIX

A NEW VOCABULARY FOR NEW IDEAS

The late Paul Harvey was a respected radio personality for many years. He became famous for revealing background information about the stories that made the news. He referred to the background feature as "The Rest of the Story." In a similar spirit, this Appendix attempts to provide background information for the new ideas and terminology that have been brought over from my previous book *The Gospel According to Relativity: Constant Value in a Changing World*. The background will be helpful for those who have not read the earlier book, and it will serve as a refresher for those who are somewhat familiar with the previous book.

1.00 SPECIAL REVELATION

Special revelation means that God has revealed himself to a particular group for a particular purpose. Special revelation in the Old Testament narrative is God's "covenant with Israel." In the New Testament narrative it is identified as the "new covenant" in Christ. Special revelation: (a) affirms the Christology of historical Christianity as well as the connection between the Old Testament and the New Testament, (b) reaffirms historical Christianity in spite of the modern trend toward religious pluralism, and (c) purges the church of its tendency to dilute the meaning of the Christ event when faced with religious pluralism.

Appendix

2.00 GENERAL REVELATION

General revelation means some aspects of God's revelation have universal impact on every person on the face of the earth—past, present, and future. Creation is general because "In the beginning God created the heavens and the earth" (Gen 1:1). The law is general because "all have sinned and fall short of the glory of God" (Rom 3:23). The Christ event is general because "God so loved the world that He gave his only begotten Son" (John 3:16). As the Son of God, Christ is the ultimate measure of value in the universe. As the constant Christ, he is the common denominator between special revelation *and* general revelation, just as the speed of light ("c") is the common denominator between special relativity *and* general relativity.

General revelation: (a) affirms the Christology of historical Christianity, (b) explains special revelation in a way that is consistent with traditional Christology, and (c) integrates special revelation and general revelation in a way that not only makes *all* people accountable to God, but also suggests the possibility that the Son's atonement and the Father's forgiveness might be available to some covenant outsiders. In other words, there is general accountability *for* sin and a general remedy *from* sin.

3.00 THEORY OF RELATIVITY OR RELATIVITY MODEL

Understanding the *general* theory of relativity as a "*general* theory of value" confirms the existence of constant value in the natural world. Constant value in science is consistent with traditional abstractions regarding constant value; that is, universal value is manifested as *love* in individual relationships and as *justice* in societal relationships. Obviously, these abstract values are applicable to secular philosophy and all world religions.

Furthermore, historical Christianity is based upon the belief that *abstract* value became *concrete* value in Jesus Christ—that is, the abstract "Word" (John 1:1) "became flesh and dwelt among us" (John 1:14), [and] "is the same yesterday, today, and forever" (Heb 13:8). The relativity model makes the case for the existence of an integrated theory of value. It is a general theory that not only accommodates Christianity, but encompasses non-Christian religions and the secular world at large.

Appendix

4.00 MOVING FRAME OF REFERENCE (THE ICON IS "?")

The moving frame of reference is the first component in Einstein's theory of relativity, and it simply means that everything in the universe is moving. For example, the earth is rotating on its axis, orbiting the sun, and hurdling through space relative to the motion of other objects in space. The philosophical idea of a moving frame of reference acknowledges the *limited* nature of human knowledge as well as the *uncertainty* that is built into the moving, changing world in which we live. The question mark icon (?) is used because it stands for the uncertainty. It gives the search for meaning a unique point of departure; that is, the departure platform is moving and changing, like everything else in the world. The situation is as if a railway passenger has suddenly discovered that both the train and the station platform are moving. The moving frame abandons the "big picture" *absolutism* of Plato, Aristotle et al., but it also rejects modern *relativism* where no "big picture" is possible. The moving frame is simply the first aspect of a new "model of understanding." It is the first leg on a three-legged stool.

5.00 UNIFORM/NON-UNIFORM MOTION (THE ICON IS "0/1")

The second component in the theory of relativity is a classification model that describes all motion as either uniform motion or non-uniform motion. Zero and one are used as icons (0/1) because the uniformity/non-uniformity model represents the lowest common denominator in the either/or classification process used in digital computers. At its simplest level, the only thing the computer does is distinguish between 0 and 1:

5.10 Uniformity

Uniformity ("0") is a primal *identity*. For example, all motion on the planet earth is uniform because of the shared rotation, but there is diversity of motion within the shared uniformity. Philosophically, a primal uniformity is seen in the oneness of each individual as well as the oneness or sameness of each group, but there is diversity within each group. I describe the "diversity" that exists *within* each uniformity as *simple* difference.

Appendix

5.20 Non-uniformity

Non-uniformity ("1") is the primal *contrast* between uniform motion and non-uniform motion. Philosophically, non-uniformity is understood as other or otherness. It is a radical or unlimited difference. Non-uniformity involves differences that are outside the oneness or sameness of uniformity. Blacks and non-Blacks have experiences that are non-uniform to each other, just as women have experiences that are non-uniform to men. Non-uniformity involves *complex* differences. Of course, the ultimate uniformity/non-uniformity is the difference that exists between the uniformity of humankind and the non-uniformity of God.

6.00 CONSTANT VALUE (THE ICON IS "C")

The constant speed of light, as the c in $E=mc^2$, is the third component in the theory of relativity. Scientifically, the free-space velocity of light (c) represents value that does not change. Regardless of the speed of a light source or the speed of one observing the light, the free-space velocity of light is *invariant*; hence "c" is the icon for constant value. Einstein integrated the moving frame, uniform/non-uniform motion, and the constant speed of light in order to produce his "general theory of relativity." It is a classic example of "the whole being greater than the sum of its parts."

I have used the general theory of relativity as an analogy for a general theory of moral and ethical values where the constant speed of light is a metaphor for eternal value. The inference is that if the speed of light does not change, then perhaps there are philosophical and/or theological values that do not change. Indeed, I would argue that the existence of constant value in science suggests the existence of eternal values in human experience. Without implying the existence of a mathematical formula, I have characterized the proposed model as follows:

moving frame + uniformity/non-uniformity + constant value = general theory
? + 0/1 + c = cValue

7.00 THE FAITH OF JESUS CHRIST

Extended discussions regarding the "faith *of* Christ" as opposed to "faith *in* Christ" are available in David H. Stern's *Jewish New Testament*

Commentary, pages 347–348 and 538–540. In support, he cites George Howard in "Romans 3:21–31 and the Inclusion of the Gentiles," *Harvard Theological Review*, 63 (1970), pages. 223–233, as well as H.E. Dana and Julius R. Mantey in *A Manual Grammar of the Greek New Testament*, The MacMillan Company, 1927; 1957 printing, pages 78–79. Contra, see E. D. Burton in *The International Critical Commentary – Galatians*, Continuum International, page 121, 1921.

Also in support, see the *NetBible* at Romans 3:22, Note 28. The NET Bible is freely available at www.bible.org. Regarding the subjective genitive vs. objective genitive debate, the translator's note says, "A decision is difficult. Though traditionally translated 'faith in Jesus Christ,' an increasing number of NT scholars are arguing that . . . *pistis Christou* and similar phrases used by Paul (here and in Rom 3:26; Gal 2:16, 20; 3:22; Eph 3:12; Phil 3:9) require the subjective genitive and mean 'Christ's faith' or 'Christ's faithfulness . . . '"[1].

THE HISTORICAL "WAVES"

8.00 THE FIRST WAVE: PREMODERN ERA

The premodern era is identified with the ancient regimes and the medieval period. Traditional ideas regarding hierarchies and absolute values had been "fixed" for many years before the transition to the modern era. Then new ideas and values began to evolve out of the Renaissance, the Protestant Reformation, the Enlightenment, modern democracy, capitalism, socialism/communism, etc. Understandably, there was a considerable overlapping of ideas between the premodern and modern eras just as there is now overlapping between the modern era and the so-called postmodern era.

---

1. Wallace, Senior Editor, *NetBible*, Rom 3:22, Note 28, para 1.

Appendix

9.00 THE SECOND WAVE: MODERN ERA

9.10 Early Modern Period

Each historical era seems to bleed over into the next period. For example, Thomas Hobbs (1588–1679), John Locke (1632–1704), and Jean Rousseau (1712–1778) are generally associated with the modern era. However, I refer to them as "early modern" because each one based his ideas on the premodern idea of a *fixed frame of reference*. They eliminated most of the philosophical and theological absolutes of the past, but they retained the idea of a fixed frame of reference. Some called it natural law, and others called it a social contract between the people and their government.

9.20 Late Modern Period

The modern perspective then shifts to a late modern perspective with the work of Soren Kierkegaard (1813–1855), Fyodor Dostoyevsky (1821–1881, Friedrich Nietzsche (1844–1900), and numerous others. Many of the earlier ideas regarding philosophy, theology, and the existence of social contracts were eventually rejected, and modern society was left with *no frame of reference*. Whereas the early modern writers had been objective and optimistic, the late modern writers were subjective and rather pessimistic. Having abandoned objectivism with its fixed frame of reference, Western civilization was left with subjectivism where there is no frame of reference. The outcome has been the widespread acceptance of moral and cultural relativism.

9.30 Postmodern or Ultramodern Period

The postmodern era is associated with the second wave even though contemporary academia has worked hard to distinguish between modernity and the so-called postmodern era. However, the power of modernism is seen in the fact that both the "pre" and "post" periods are identified in relation to the modern era. Postmodernism merely carries modernity to its logical (or illogical) conclusion; that is, postmodernism says there are no eternal values and every thing is changing and evolving. I agree with

Appendix

Thomas Oden that the so-called postmodern mentality is "ultramodern" rather than "postmodern."[2]

Postmodern writers like Jacque Derrida (1930–2004), Michel Foucault (1926–1984), and others merely took the next logical step. They discredited the ideas of earlier writers, discounted the reliability of the written word, and left each reader to interpret each "text" (the linguistic content of any communication) in light of his or her own experience. The "meaning" of the text is left up to each reader and especially to literary critics who are the professional readers. The critics are the "wise ones" who deconstruct the author's hidden agenda and expose the mother lode of bias to the light of day. Admittedly, each text has a context, but postmodern critics are focused on the idea of a "subtext"—a hidden meaning that has allegedly "already arrived" before the reader begins to read.

10.00 THE THIRD WAVE: THE NEXT ERA

Relativity theory moves the conversation forward. It acknowledges the existence of a *moving frame of reference* that reflects the disorder that often accompanies human effort. In fact, when the "moving frame of reference" is standing alone, it looks a lot like having "no frame of reference."

However, relativity uses *uniformity/non-uniformity* as a classification model (sameness/difference, self/other, etc.) to impose linguistic order for both private and public discourse. The strength of the model is that it is inclusive, non-discriminatory, and descriptive (what is) rather than prescriptive (what ought to be). There can be no inherent preference for or against one ideology because the model is reversible. In other words, the insider's uniformity is actually non-uniformity from the outsider's perspective. If we stop the analysis at this point, there is no constant value because there is "*no* frame of reference."

Relativity is value-based because *constant value* is superimposed on philosophy and theology, much as the constant speed of light in $E=mc^2$ is superimposed on the theory of relativity. In the final analysis, non-Christian religions and most forms of secularism are value-based. That is, they agree with the universality of constant value as seen in its abstract form— in the *love* that exists in individual relationships and in the *justice* that is needed in social, political, and economic relationships. For Christians,

2. Oden, *After Modernity . . . What?*, 77.

the universality of constant value is "made flesh" in the person of Jesus Christ. Abstract value becomes concrete value in the "constant Christ."

11.00 ONLINE BOOK REVIEW BY DR. L. RUSS BUSH (1944-2008)

James W. Geiger. *The Gospel According to Relativity: Constant Value in a Changing World*. USA: Xulon Press, 2005, Pages 223

Jim Geiger graduated from Stetson University and Stetson Law School, studied at American University, the FBI Academy, and Knox Seminary, and practices law in Fort Lauderdale FL. His special interest for several years has been Christian Faith and Science. This book offers what Jim hopes is a viable alternative to traditional approaches.

We all know how strong the pressure is to yield to naturalism and post-modernism, but Geiger argues that Einstein's theory of relativity is not relativism (a philosophical theory). The key component in relativity is the constant speed of light. It is an unusual component in that it remains the same no matter what else changes. This means that science is not devoid of constant value, as is so often supposed. Postmodernism is a false idea. Relativity is not relativism.

The text of the book actually covers the history of philosophy in a very creative way, working from a traditional fixed frame of reference, through the modern/postmodern era where there is no frame of reference, to a moving frame of reference that is the first component for a new "model of understanding" for the 21st Century. The second component is a classification duality as with male/female, black/white, etc., which imposes linguistic order on a world that is continuingly moving and changing. But this does not lead to a relativized theory of truth because the model's third component, the constant speed of light, confirms the existence of constant value. Part One applies the model to Christian philosophy where the constant speed of light reminds us that the constant Christ is "the same, yesterday, and today, and forever."

In Part Two, Geiger replicates the same model for secularism and other world religions. Whereas in Part One constant value is "made flesh" and "dwells among us"—in Part Two constant value manifests itself as abstract instead of as incarnate, that is, as love in personal relationships and as justice is societal relationships. Geiger takes a strong position favoring

Christianity as the true source of value. He ends the book with a statement about the next forty years: Can we as a society say yes to a spiritual plane that acknowledges the uncertainties of the present era, promotes nondiscriminatory discourse in the public square, and articulates constant value in a way that has appeal for all people? A voice is calling in the wilderness; clear the way for the Lord.

This review is not an adequate summary of the content of the book. The book contains many insights into the strengths and weaknesses of traditional interpretations of Western philosophy. Generally I find him to be a valuable guide in his analysis, creative in his alternatives, and certainly worth reading.

I find the basic thesis of the book to be that in physics and the other hard sciences as well as theology and philosophy, nothing makes any sense unless there is a spiritual referent that is invariant. Just as the speed of light represents constant value in science, the constant Christ is the constant reality in Christian theology. I would emphasize that the key is to understand that the constant Christ was incarnate, was tempted in all ways, as are we, and was not robotic in his submission to the Father. That insight saves Christianity from being a deterministic system (though Christ remains the final truth, the only way, and the source of all life.)

> L. Russ Bush, Director
> Center for Faith and Culture
> Southeastern Seminary
> Wake Forest, NC 27588

Bibliography

Augustine. *The Confessions of Saint Augustine*, Translated by E.B. Pusey. New York: Touchstone Books, 1997.
Bellah, Robert, et al. *Habits of the Heart.* New York: Perennial Lib, Harper & Row, 1985.
Berry, George Ricker. *The Interlinear Greek-English New Testament.* Grand Rapids: Regency Reference Library, Zondervan Imprint, 1990.
Bonhoeffer, Dietrich. *The Cost of Discipleship.* New York: Macmillan, 1949.
Burson, Scott R. and Jerry L. Walls. *C.S. Lewis & Francis Schaeffer: Lessons for a New Century from the Most Influential Apologists of Our Time.* Downer Grove: InterVarsity Press, 1998.
Bush, L. Russ. *The Advancement: Keeping the Faith in an Evolutionary Age.* Nashville: Broadman & Holman Publishers, 2003.
Dawkins, Richard. *The God Delusion.* New York: Houghton Mifflin Co., 2006.
Derrida, Jacques. "Difference." *Margins of Philosophy.* Translated by Alan Bass, Chicago: University of Chicago Press, 1982.
———. "Plato's Pharmacy." *Dissemination.* Translator Barbara Johnson, Chicago: University of Chicago Press, 1983.
Detweiler, Robert. "No Place to Start" *Religion & Intellectual Life,* New Rochelle: ARIL Winter, 1988.
Eagleton, Terry. *Literary Theory: An Introduction.* Minneapolis: University of Minnesota Press, 1983.
Erickson, Millard J. *Postmodernizing the Faith.* Grand Rapids: Baker Books, 1998.
Geiger, James W. *The Gospel According to Relativity: Constant Value in a Changing World.* Longwood: Xulon Press, 2005.
Gilkey, Langdon. "A Retrospective Glance at My Work." In *The Whirlwind in Culture,* edited by Donald W. Musser et al., 1–35, Bloomington: Meyer-Stone Books, 1988.
Goldstein, Rebecca. *Incompleteness: The Proof and Paradox of Kurt Godel.* New York: W.W. Norton & Company, 2005.
Green Sr., Jay P. *The Interlinear Bible.* Peabody: Hendrickson Publishers, 1985.
Gundry, Robert. "Tom's Targum." (April 2012). No pages. Online: http://www.booksandculture.com/articles/2012/mayjun/tomstargum.html.
Hawking, Stephen W. *A Brief History of Time.* New York: Bantam Books, 1988.
Jenkins, Philip. *The Next Christendom: The Coming of Global Christianity.* New York: Oxford University Press, 2002.

Bibliography

Jordan, Mark D. "Augustine." In *The Cambridge Dictionary of Philosophy*. Cambridge University Press, NY, (1995).

Kaufmann, Walter. *Existentialism from Dostoyevsky to Sartre*. New York: Meridian Books, 1957.

Kierkegaard, Soren. *"The Journals (1834-1842)."* Translated by Alexander Dru. *A Kierkegaard Anthology*. Edited by Robert Bretall, New York: The Modern Library, 1946.

Lewis, C. S. *Mere Christianity*. New York: Harper-San Francisco, 2001.

Ludwig, Karl E. "Max Planck." In *The Cambridge Dictionary of Scientists*, New York: Cambridge Press, 1996.

Miller, Arthur. *Death of a Salesman*. New York: Penguin, 1998.

Nietzsche, Friedrich. *Basic Writings of Nietzsche*. Translated by Walter Kaufmann, New York: The Modern Library, 1968.

Novak, David. "The Mind of Maimonides." *First Things*. New York: Institute on Religion and Public Life, February 1999.

Oden, Thomas C. *After Modernity ... What?* Grand Rapids: Zondervan Publishing House, 1992.

Palmer, Donald. *Looking At Philosophy*. Mountain View: Mayfield Publishing Company, 1988.

Rawls, John. *A Theory of Justice*. Cambridge: Belknap Press of Harvard University Press, 2005.

Schaeffer, Francis. *The God Who Is There*. Dowers Grove: InterVarsity Press, 1968.

Smith, James K.A. "Teaching a Calvinist to Dance." *Christianity Today*, Carol Stream, IL, (2008) On line: http://www.christianitytoday.com/ct/2008/may/25.42.html?start=3.

Stern, David H. *Jewish New Testament Commentary*. Clarksville: Jewish New Testament Publications, 1992.

———. *Complete Jewish Bible*. Translated by David H. Stern, Clarksville: Jewish New Testament Publications, 1998.

Stewart, Matthew. *The Courtier and the Heretic: Leibniz, Spinoza, And The Fate of God In The Modern World*. New York: Norton & Company, 2006.

Toffler, Alvin. *The Third Wave*. New York: Bantam Books, 1981.

Twain, Mark. *Following the Equator*, Stilwell: Digireads Publishing, 2008.

Wallace, Daniel. Senior New Testament Editor of *Net Bible*. Biblical Studies Press, 2005. No pages. Online: http://bible.org/netbible/Rom3:22 Note 28.

Yeats, William Butler. "The Second Coming." *Classics of Western Thought: The Modern World*. Edited by Charles Hirschfeld, New York: Harcourt, Brace & World, 1968.

Zodhiates, Spiros. *The Complete Word Study New Testament With Parallel Greek KJV*. Chattanooga: AMG Publishers, 1992.

———. *The Complete Word Study Old Testament KJV*. Chattanooga: AMG Publishers, 1994.

www.ingramcontent.com/pod-product-compliance
Lightning Source LLC
Chambersburg PA
CBHW062027220426
43662CB00010B/1511